636,1007

D1390048

CENTRE
S

A STUDENT WORKBOOK
FOR
BHS STAGE TWO

A STUDENT WORKBOOK
FOR
BHS STAGE TWO

MAXINE CAVE

BHSSM+T

J. A. ALLEN
London

British Library Cataloguing-in-Publication Data.
A catalogue record for this book is available from the British Library.

ISBN 0 85131 826 6

© J. A. Allen 2000

No part of this book may be reproduced, stored in a retrieval system, or trans-mitted, in any form or by any means, electronic, mechanical, photocopying, recording or otherwise, without the prior permission of the publisher. All rights reserved.

Published in Great Britain in 2000 by
J. A. Allen
an imprint of Robert Hale Ltd
Clerkenwell House
45–47 Clerkenwell Green
London EC1R 0HT

Typesetting and production: Bill Ireson
Colour photography: Bob Langrish
Illustrations: Maggie Raynor
Cover design: Nancy Lawrence
Printed in Singapore by Kyodo Printing Co (S'pore) Pte Ltd

For Basym

Contents

	Introduction	*1*
1	Grooming and Care of the Horse	3
2	Tack and Clothing	10
3	The Foot and Shoeing	28
4	Stable Design	37
5	Clipping and Trimming	41
6	The Horse's Health	53
7	The Horse's Digestive System	61
8	The Skeleton	67
9	Horse Behaviour	74
10	Fittening	83
11	Grassland Management	93
12	Feeding and Watering	102
13	Travelling	112
14	Lungeing	122
15	General Knowledge	126
	Exam Notes	*131*
	Answers to the Questions	*143*

Introduction

This question-and-answer workbook will not guarantee that you pass your exam. But it will improve your chances of success and build on the work you have done on the way to the big day.

The questions are representative of those which a candidate may be asked during a BHS Stage Two examination. Each examiner, of course, has his or her own way of phrasing a question, but the questions in this book are of the general type asked.

Some questions may appear very simple, asking the candidate to "state the obvious". Their inclusion here is intended to demonstrate that examiners are not asking candidates for complicated or in-depth answers at this level; they simply want to know that each candidate has acquired the basic knowledge and experience required at Stage Two and that the candidate is showing some progression from the previous level.

In the same way, the example answers to the questions have been selected to demonstrate the depth of knowledge sought by the examiner. Students may come up with answers that differ from those selected here. This does not necessarily mean that the answers the students have given are incorrect; to some of the questions, there can be more than one answer.

At the centre of the book students will find a section intended to prove that examiners are human too! Most people taking the exam are nervous on the day and may think that examiners are trying to catch them out. They are not; don't forget that all BHS examiners have taken and passed this exam at some stage in their career so they do know how you are feeling. So, read this section first if you want to know what the exam consists of, how it will be conducted, what is expected of you, and how the examiners will arrive at their decision.

Good luck on the day.

MAXINE CAVE

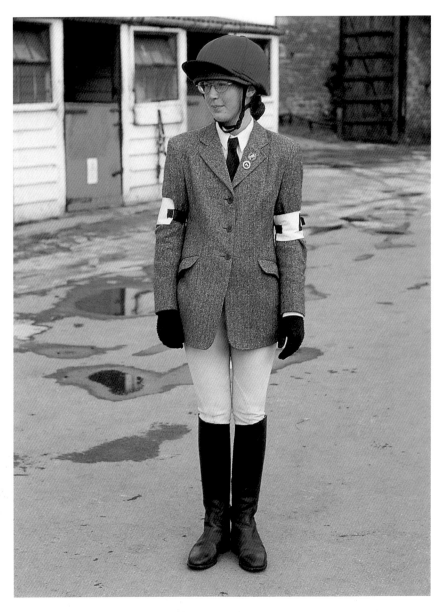

A candidate prepares to take the BHS examination

This photograph was taken under examination conditions at The Talland School of Equitation

1 Grooming and Care of the Horse

Questions

1. Identify the three pieces of equipment, A to C, illustrated below.

....

....

....

....

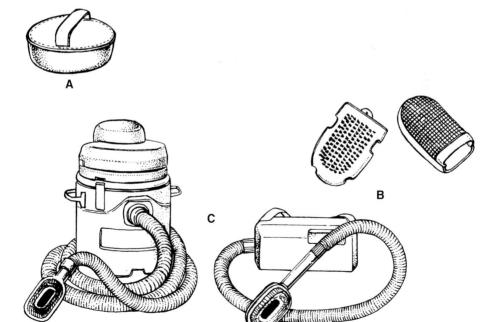

2. What is a wisp?

   ....

3. What is a wisp used for?

   ....

   ....

4. Wisping may be referred to by different names. What other names might some people use?

   ....

   ....

   ....

5. What do you understand by the term "strapping"?

   ....

   ....

   ....

6. Describe the modern types of wisp now available.

   ....

   ....

   ....

   ....

7. The horse below appears to be a stabled horse with a summer coat. What tools would you use to give the horse a thorough grooming and what routine would you follow?

....

....

....

....

....

....

....

8. Explain the procedure for wisping a horse.

    ....

    ....

    ....

    ....

    ....

    ....

9. What type of work might a horse be doing, if it would benefit from being wisped?

    ....

    ....

    ....

    ....

    ....

10. In what circumstances might you wisp a horse which is not in work?

    ....

    ....

    ....

    ....

11. What is quartering?

....

....

12. When and why would you quarter a horse?

....

....

....

....

....

13. List and explain the reasons for grooming.

....

....

....

....

....

....

....

....

14. If your horse has just returned from a period of strenuous work, such as hunting, or a cross-country competition, there are certain procedures to follow to ensure that you take good care of it. Some questions on these procedures are listed, (i) to (vi), on this and the opposite page. Write an answer to each question.

(i)   What action should you take first?

....

....

....

....

....

(ii)   What particular points will you check for?

....

....

....

(iii)   How do you you ensure that the horse quenches its thirst?

....

....

....

....

(iv)   How will the procedure differ from summer to winter
        weather conditions?

....

....

....

....

(v)   What particular injuries will you carefully check for?

....

....

....

....

....

(vi)   What will you check about the horse's feet?

....

....

....

....

2 Tack and Clothing

Questions

1. Describe some different types of straps and fastenings used on horse turnout rugs.

   ....

   ....

   ....

2. Identify the type of roller worn by this horse.

   ....

   ....

3. In what circumstances might you use an anti-cast roller?.

    ....

    ....

    ....

    ....

4. How might you come to realise that your horse was not comfortable in its stable rug?

    ....

    ....

    ....

5. Some modern stable rugs are designed to wick away moisture. In what circumstances would this type of rug be particularly useful?

    ....

    ....

    ....

6. How often would you need to wash your horse's rug?

    ....

    ....

    ....

    ....

7. How would you go about cleaning a turnout rug?

....

....

....

8. How do you store rugs that are not in use?

....

....

....

9. Outline the procedure for bandaging a horse's legs for warmth and protection.

....

....

....

10. Why should gamgee, or "fybagee", be used under bandages?

....

....

....

....

....

....

11. Describe the bandages that can be used without padding underneath. Explain why they can be used like this.

....

....

....

....

....

....

....

12. When would you need to bandage a horse for warmth?

....

....

....

....

13. When would you need to bandage a horse for protection?

....

....

....

....

....

14. Equipment set out for examination candidates to identify. Name the boot illustrated here that a horse wears on its foot rather than on its leg.

....

15. What are overreach boots? Explain what they are for.

....

....

....

....

....

16. Are overreach boots referred to by any other name and if so what is it?

....

....

17. In what circumstances might you use overreach boots on the horse's hind feet?

....

....

....

....

....

18. What injuries may occur if the overreach boots are of a poor fit?

....

....

....

....

....

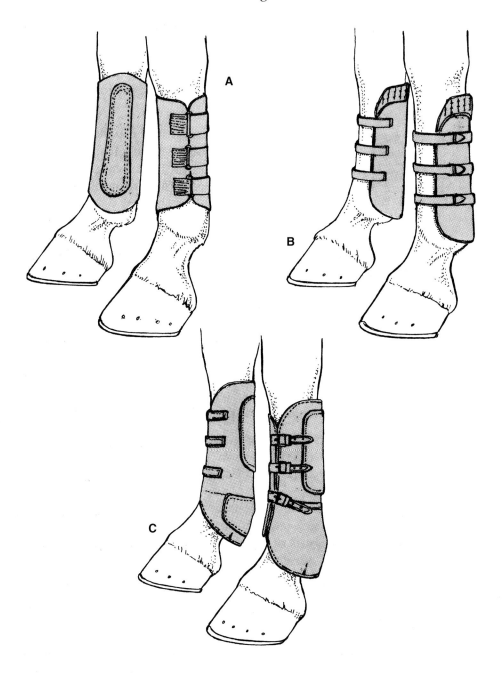

19. Look at the illustration on the opposite page. Identify the boots, A to C.

....

....

....

....

....

20. There are many different designs of overreach boot. Which type would you prefer and why?

....

....

....

21. Why and when would you use simple brushing boots?

....

....

....

22. In what circumstances would you avoid using brushing boots?

....

....

....

23. What injuries may occur if brushing boots are ill-fitting?

....

....

....

....

....

24. Saddles may be narrow, medium or wide fits. To which part of the saddle does this refer?

....

25. Which part of the horse is affected by the width fitting of the saddle?

....

....

26. If a saddle is a 17 inch, where is this measurement taken?

....

27. What measurement of saddle would most adults use?

....

....

....

....

28. Explain how you would go about fitting a saddle.

....

....

....

....

....

29. Is it necessary for a rider to try out a new saddle before making a decision on fit, and if so why?

....

....

....

30. Where would you look for signs of injury if you came across a horse with an ill-fitting saddle?

....

....

....

31. In what different sizes are bridles made?

....

....

....

32. Explain how you would go about fitting a bridle.

....

....

....

....

....

33. Where would the most likely injuries be if a bridle was a poor fit?

....

....

....

....

....

34. What tack is required to equip a horse for lungeing exercise?

....

....

....

....

....

....

35. Identify the tack illustrated above.

....

36. Why is it advisable to fit boots to all four legs of the horse for lungeing?

....

....

37. Give reasons for and against using a saddle for lungeing exercise.

....

....

....

....

38. Describe how the lunge cavesson and bridle should be fitted together on the horse.

....

....

....

....

....

39. Describe how the side reins should be attached to the saddle.

....

....

....

....

....

....

40. Explain what guidelines you follow when adjusting the side reins?

....

....

....

....

41. To which ring on the lunge cavesson do you attach the lunge line?

   ....

   ....

42. Which parts of the saddle, bridle, boots and other accessories, should be checked every day for safety?

   ....

   ....

   ....

43. Explain a situation in which a martingale or breastplate might be used when lungeing.

   ....

   ....

   ....

   ....

44. Explain how to fit a martingale.

   ....

   ....

   ....

   ....

   ....

45. Explain how to fit a breastplate.

....

....

....

....

....

....

46. Give a brief description of three different types of boot, used to protect horses' legs.

....

....

....

....

....

....

47. Explain the use and purpose of the three types of boot you have described.

....

....

....

48. What injuries might a horse sustain from poor fitting protective boots?

....

....

....

....

49. What guidelines do you follow for fitting a bit?

....

....

....

50. Explain how the different thickness of the mouthpiece of a bit has a different effect on the horse.

....

....

....

....

51. Which areas of the head and mouth may different bits apply pressure to?

....

....

....

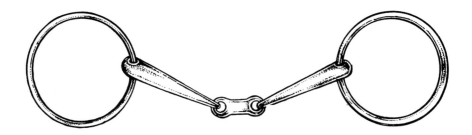

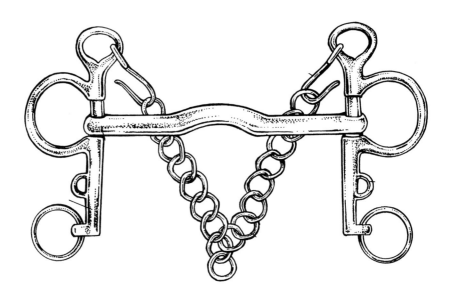

52. Identify these two bits.

....

....

53. Name the five main families of different bits.

....

....

....

....

....

3 The Foot and Shoeing

Questions

1. Name the farrier's tools illustrated below.

    ....

    ....

    ....

    ....

    ....

2. The farrier will begin by removing the horse's old shoes. Which tools will the farrier use to do this?

....

3. Describe what the farrier does with the tools in order to remove the shoes.

....

....

....

....

....

....

4. How does the farrier hold up a front foot of the horse in order to have both hands free?

....

....

....

5. How does the farrier hold up a hind foot of the horse in order to have both hands free?

....

....

....

6. What is this farrier doing?

....

....

7. What is the tripod used for?

   ....

   ....

   ....

8. What is the rasp used for?

   ....

   ....

   ....

9. What is the drawing knife used for?

   ....

   ....

   ....

10. What are the hoof cutters used for?

   ....

   ....

   ....

11. How many nails are usually used to secure the horse's shoe?

   ....

   ....

12. What are the clenching tongs used for?

....

....

....

13. What is the buffer used for?

....

....

14. How often should a horse be shod?

....

....

....

15. What factors contribute to the length of time left between new sets of shoes?

....

....

....

....

....

....

....

16. What problems might result if the horse's shoes are left on too long?

....

....

....

....

....

....

17. Explain the function of the horse's foot.

....

....

....

....

....

18. Why is it necessary to have horses shod?

....

....

....

....

....

19. Look at the illustration on the opposite page. Name the parts of the horse's foot, A to Z.

....

....

....

....

....

....

....

....

....

....

....

....

....

....

....

....

....

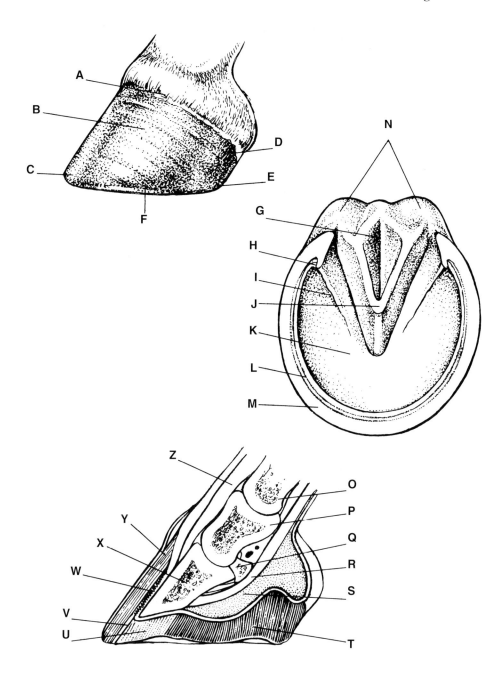

20. Describe the process you would use to remove a horse's shoe. Name the tools you would need for the procedure.

....

....

....

....

....

....

....

....

....

....

....

4 Stable Design

Questions

1. How big does a stable for a 14hh pony, ideally, need to be?

   ....

   ....

2. How big does a stable for a 16hh horse, ideally, need to be?

   ....

   ....

3. How big does a stable for an in-foal mare, ideally, need to be?

   ....

   ....

4. What fixtures and fittings would you like to have in a horse's stable?

   ....

   ....

   ....

   ....

   ....

   ....

5. Give reasons for your chosen fixtures.

....

....

....

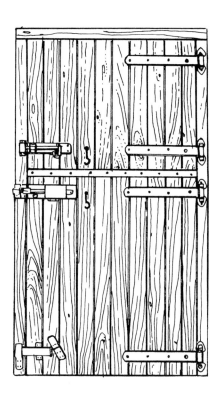

6. List four good features on the stable door above.

....

....

....

....

7. Where would you position a tie-up ring in the stable and why?

   ....

   ....

8. What general factors should be considered when choosing a location for a stable?

   ....

   ....

   ....

9. What key features should be incorporated into the floor of the stable to make it suitable for a horse?

   ....

   ....

   ....

10. Name three different types of roofing material and explain the pros and cons of each.

   ....

   ....

   ....

   ....

   ....

   ....

11. How high and wide should a stable door be?

....

....

....

12. Why is head room important in the stable, and how can it be most effectively provided?

....

....

....

....

5 Clipping and Trimming

Questions

1. Why are horses clipped?

....

....

....

....

2. How would you introduce a horse to clippers, if it had not been clipped before?

....

....

....

....

3. How would you prepare a horse, familiar with clipping, prior to starting the clip?

....

....

....

....

4. Look at the opposite page. Name the different types of clip, A to E, illustrated.

....

....

....

....

....

....

5. What sort of area is most suitable for clipping?

....

....

....

....

....

6. What equipment will you need for yourself before you begin clipping?

....

....

....

....

A

B

C

D

E

7. What checks and preparation will you make to the clippers before you begin clipping?

....

....

....

....

8. How long will it usually take to hunter clip a well-behaved horse?

....

9. Whilst clipping the horse, what attention will you need to give to the clippers in order to keep them working properly?

....

....

10. How many clips will a sharp set of blades be able to do, and what will it depend on?

....

....

....

11. What is meant by a "circuit breaker"? Why is it so important when clippers are being used?

....

....

12. Describe how you go about starting off the clip and explain why.

   ....

   ....

   ....

   ....

13. In what month of the year are you most likely to give a horse its first clip of the season?

   ....

   ....

14. In what circumstances might you clip a horse during the summer?

   ....

   ....

   ....

   ....

15. In what way could an assistant help while you are clipping?

   ....

   ....

   ....

   ....

16. If a horse is frightened, or fidgets, when it is being clipped, what methods of restraint could be used?

....

....

....

....

17. Why might a horse become frightened of being clipped?

....

....

....

18. Describe some of the ways in which the clip is made to look neat and professional.

....

....

....

19. What can you do to finish off the horse once the clip is complete?

....

....

....

....

20. What points to do with the horse's comfort must you be aware of during the clipping process?

....

....

....

....

....

21. How should you store the clippers and the blades after use?

....

....

....

22. What parts of the horse can be trimmed using scissors and comb?

....

....

....

23. Describe how you go about trimming these different areas.

....

....

....

....

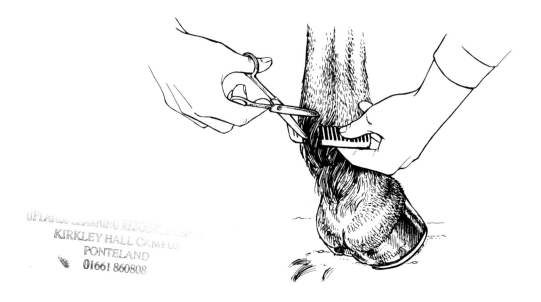

UPLANDS LEARNING RESOURCE CENTRE
KIRKLEY HALL CAMPUS
PONTELAND
01661 860808

24. What is being done above – and why?

....

....

....

....

....

....

....

....

....

25. Some people disagree with trimming certain areas of a horse. Which areas are these and why?

....

....

....

....

26. Which types of horse or pony are not usually trimmed at all?

....

....

....

....

27. How do you go about pulling a horse's mane?

....

....

....

28. Why do some horses have their manes pulled?

....

....

....

....

29. In what sort of condition does the horse's mane need to be for plaiting?

....

....

....

30. How do you go about preparing for plaiting a horse's mane?

....

....

....

....

31. Do you begin plaiting from the poll, or the withers, and why?

....

....

32. In what sort of condition does the horse's tail need to be for the purpose of plaiting?

....

....

....

....

....

33. How do you go about preparing for plaiting a horse's tail?

....

....

....

....

34. Give a brief explanation of the plaiting procedure for manes and tails.

....

....

....

....

....

....

....

....

35. How do you go about pulling a horse's tail?

....

....

....

....

36. Why is the assistant holding up the horse's tail?

....

....

....

....

....

....

....

6 The Horse's Health

UPLANDS LEARNING RESOURCE CENTRE
KIRKLEY HALL CAMPUS
PONTELAND
01661 860808

Questions

1. List ten points that indicate a horse is in good health.

....

....

....

....

....

....

....

....

....

....

....

....

....

....

....

2. List ten points that indicate a horse is not in good health.

....

....

....

....

....

....

....

....

....

....

3. What preventive measures can be taken on a regular basis to help
    ensure that the horse remains in good health?

....

....

....

....

....

....

4. What records should you keep, and why, with regard to your horse's health?

....

....

....

....

5. What is being done to the horse below?

....

....

....

....

6. What factors might cause you to call out a vet to your horse?

....

....

....

....

....

7. Explain the principles of nursing a sick horse?

....

....

....

....

....

8. Explain how you detect lameness in the horse.

....

....

....

....

....

....

9. Describe what you see that leads you to think that this horse is
    healthy?

    ....

    ....

    ....

    ....

    ....

    ....

10. How often should a horse be wormed?

....

....

11. How often should a horse have its teeth checked?

....

....

12. What signs may indicate your horse's teeth need attention?

....

....

....

13. If your horse has been lame or sick, how will you decide when you can ride it again?

....

....

....

....

14. Why do horses need their teeth rasped?

....

....

....

15. What might happen if you do not worm your horse at regular intervals?

....

....

....

....

16. How would you treat a girth gall?

....

....

....

17. How would you treat a sore mouth?

....

....

....

18. How would you treat a superficial cut on the leg?

....

....

....

....

19. How would you treat an area of heat and swelling on a limb?

....

....

....

....

....

....

....

....

7 The Horse's Digestive System

Questions

1. Name the five parts of the horse's digestive system and describe the function of each. Start with the first part, the horse's lips.

   ....

   ....

   ....

   ....

   ....

   ....

   ....

   ....

2. Describe the main features and functions of the stomach.

   ....

   ....

   ....

   ....

   ....

   ....

3. Describe the small and large intestines and explain the function of both.

....

....

....

....

....

....

....

....

....

....

....

....

4. What is the alimentary canal?

....

....

....

....

5. Name the internal organs, A to G, in the illustration below.

....

....

....

....

....

....

....

....

UPLANDS LEARNING RESOURCE CENTRE
KIRKLEY.HALL.CAMPUS
PONTELAND
01661 860808

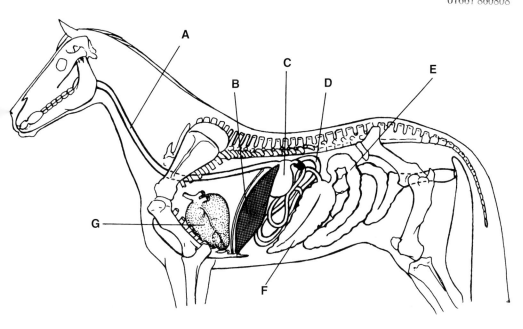

6. Name the internal organs, A to E
   in this illustration.

....

....

....

....

....

....

....

....

A

B

C

D

E

7. Name two accessory organs that aid digestion.

....

....

8. What do these two accessory organs do?

....

....

....

9. What are carbohydrates for?

....

....

....

....

10. What are proteins for?

....

....

....

....

11. Can horses regurgitate food or be sick? If not, why not?

....

....

....

....

....

....

....

....

12. Name the parts of the digestive system, A to K, illustrated below.

....

....

....

....

....

8 The Skeleton

Questions

1. Why is it helpful to know about the horse's skeleton?

   ....

   ....

   ....

   ....

2. Why is the skeleton essential?

   ....

   ....

   ....

   ....

3. Name and give examples of the three different types of joint.

   ....

   ....

   ....

   ....

   ....

   ....

4. What is the appendicular skeleton?

....

....

....

....

....

5. What is the function of the skull?

....

....

....

....

....

6. What are the vertebrae? What do they protect?

....

....

....

....

....

....

7. How many pairs of ribs does the horse have? Why are some called "true" and others "false"?

....

....

....

....

....

8. Does the horse have a collar bone to which the front limbs are attached? If not, to what are they attached?

....

....

....

....

....

9. What is cartilage?

....

....

....

....

....

10. Look at the illustration on the opposite page. Name the horse's bones, A to T. Write your answer below and continue on the opposite page if necessary.

....

....

....

....

....

....

....

....

....

....

....

....

....

....

....

....

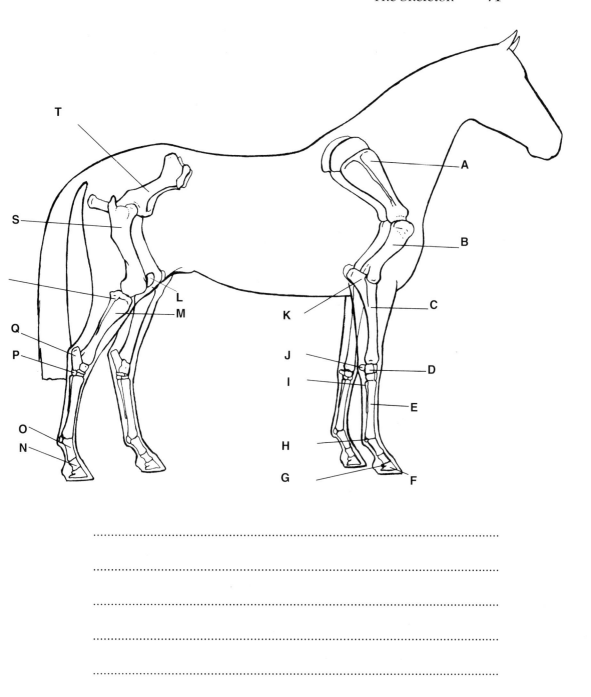

11. Name the horse's bones, A to F, in the illustration below.

....

....

....

....

....

....

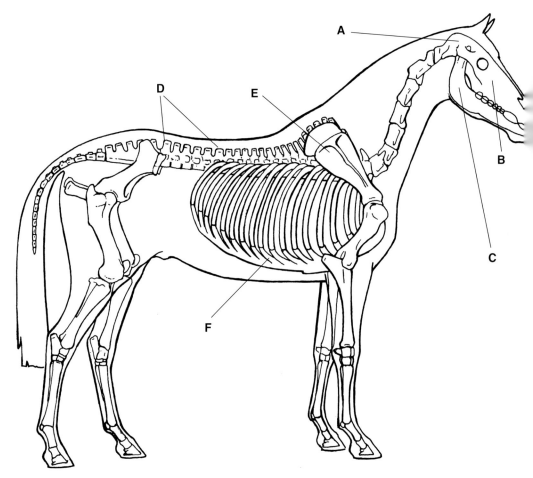

12. If you compare the horse's limbs with those of a human being, which joints are the stifle, the hock, and the knee?

....

....

....

....

....

13. What does the axial skeleton consist of?

....

....

....

14. Name the five different sections of vertebrae which make up the horse's spine. State how many vertebrae there are in each section.

....

....

....

....

....

....

....

9 Horse Behaviour

Questions

1. When you are feeding a group of horses in the field, what aspect of the horse's natural behaviour may become evident?

   ....

   ....

   ....

   ....

   ....

2. When you are feeding hay to a group of horses in the field, how can you reduce the problems caused by the horses' instinctive behaviour?

   ....

   ....

   ....

   ....

3. What do you understand by the term "pecking order"?

   ....

   ....

   ....

4. What different weather conditions would prompt you to bring
    your horse in from the field, and why?

    ....

    ....

    ....

5. When several horses are kept together in the field, why might
    you sometimes separate mares from geldings?

    ....

    ....

    ....

6. In what circumstances would you expect to see horses lying
    down in the field?

    ....

    ....

    ....

7. In what circumstances would you be worried if your horse was
    lying down in the field?

    ....

    ....

    ....

    ....

8. Describe the behaviour of these two horses.

....

....

....

....

9. What behaviour would you expect to see if a horse was left alone in the field?

....

....

10. Why would the horse behave in that way?

UPLANDS LEARNING RESOURCE CENTRE
KIRKLEY HALL CAMPUS
PONTELAND
01661 260000

....

....

....

11. What sort of behaviour is being displayed by the two horses below? And in what circumstances is such behaviour seen?

....

....

....

....

12. When you introduce a new horse into a field with an established group what behaviour would you expect to see?

....

....

....

....

....

13. What steps would you take to ensure your horse is happy and relaxed in its stabled environment?

....

....

....

....

....

14. How will you know if your horse is feeling relaxed and secure in the stable?

....

....

....

....

....

15. What behaviour would you see if a horse was unhappy in its stable?

....

....

....

....

....

16. Explain why some horses may be happy stabled in a certain part of the yard, while others may not be?

....

....

....

....

....

17. What sort of behaviour will you see if a new horse is distressed when it arrives and is put in a stable?

....

....

....

....

....

18. What sort of behaviour will make you cautious when you approach a stabled horse?

....

....

....

....

....

....

19. Explain how stabling a horse goes against its natural instincts.

....

....

....

....

....

20. How can you gain the confidence of a nervous stabled horse?

....

....

....

....

....

21. What would you expect to see if a loud bang was suddenly heard by the horses grazing in this field?

....

....

....

....

....

....

....

....

22. When riding out, what behaviour would lead you to say that your horse was feeling fresh and excited?

....

....

....

....

23. How would ill-fitting tack affect the ridden horse?

....

....

....

....

24. What is the best way to gain a horse's confidence, at all times, in the stable or in the field?

....

....

....

....

....

10 Fittening

Questions

1. If your horse has had a couple of month's holiday at grass in the summer, what first steps will you take when you begin a fitness programme aiming to prepare the horse for regular daily riding and perhaps some light hunting?

....

....

....

....

....

....

....

2. What differences are there between preparing a horse for a fitness programme after it has had a summer holiday in comparison to a winter holiday?

....

....

....

....

....

3. Why is it best not to clip a horse at the very beginning of a fitness programme?

    ....

    ....

    ....

4. Describe the type and amount of work you will give your horse in its first week.

    ....

    ....

    ....

    ....

    ....

5. Describe what you could do to help prevent sores developing when tack is first used again on a horse's soft skin.

    ....

    ....

6. Explain why working a horse uphill is so beneficial as part of a fitness programme.

    ....

    ....

    ....

7. When might it be useful to exercise your horse in this way?

    ....

    ....

    ....

    ....

8. What parts of the horse are you developing and changing during
   a fitness programme?

    ....

    ....

9. When a horse is recovering from illness or injury, what special care must you take when bringing it back into work?

   ....

   ....

   ....

10. What is meant by "outline"? How important is it during a fitness programme designed for general riding?

   ....

   ....

   ....

   ....

11. What injuries could result from working a horse in heavy going, on the roads, and over stony or uneven ground?

   ....

   ....

   ....

   ....

12. How long will you work your horse for each day of the fitness programme?

   ....

   ....

13. Is it best to split up your horse's work into one or more sessions each day? What does the decision depend upon?

....

....

....

....

....

14. At what point will you introduce canter work?

....

....

15. Will you introduce any schooling work, and if so why?

....

....

....

....

16. Is it necessary to give your horse a day off each week? If so, why?

....

....

....

17. Is the horse illustrated below working in a good outline? Explain your answer.

....

....

....

....

....

....

....

18. Explain the importance of "warming up".

....

....

....

19. How many weeks of a fitness programme will it take to prepare a horse for regular daily riding and perhaps some light hunting? What will it depend upon?

....

....

....

....

....

....

....

20. How will your horse's feeding routine change during the fitness programme?

....

....

....

....

21. When working your horse through the fitness programme what ailments may you have to deal with?

....

....

....

....

22. After a horse has had a period of hard work – such as hunting or a cross-country competition – what action is necessary before it is returned to its stable?

....

....

....

....

....

....

23. Explain how you ensure that your horse has quenched its thirst.

....

....

....

....

....

24. What else should you do to ensure that your horse is well cared for after this period of hard work?

....

....

....

....

25. Is there any special attention your horse should have the next day?

....

....

....

....

26. How might lungeing a horse help with a fitness programme?

....

....

....

27. List the main points to be followed when "roughing off" a horse for a winter holiday. Explain your answer.

....

....

....

....

28. List the main points to be followed when "roughing off" a horse for a summer holiday. Explain your answer.

....

....

....

....

....

....

....

11 Grassland Management

UPLANDS LEARNING RESOURCE CENTRE
KIRKLEY HALL CAMP
PONTELAND
01661 860808

Questions

1. What condition should your horse paddocks be in if they are to provide good grazing? How will you maintain them?

   ....

   ....

   ....

   ....

   ....

   ....

   ....

2. Outline the fencing requirements for field-kept horses.

   ....

   ....

   ....

   ....

   ....

   ....

   ....

3. Look at the two pictures on the opposite page. Describe the good and bad points of the fencing shown.

   ....

   ....

   ....

   ....

   ....

   ....

   ....

   ....

4. Describe the features you would look for in a good gate for a horse paddock.

   ....

   ....

   ....

   ....

5. What is the most efficient way of providing water for horses in the field?

   ....

   ....

   ....

6. How often should you check the horse's water supply? What are you checking for at different times of the year?

   ....

   ....

   ....

   ....

   ....

7. What do horses need shelter from when living out in the field?

   ....

   ....

   ....

   ....

   ....

   ....

8. How can horses be provided with shelter?

   ....

   ....

   ....

   ....

   ....

9. What is this plant? Is it poisonous?

....

....

....

....

10. Describe foxgloves.

....

....

....

11. Describe yew.

....

....

12. Describe laburnum.

....

....

13. Describe deadly nightshade.

....

....

14. Look at the illustration on the opposite page. Identify those plants, A to G, which are poisonous. Describe where you are most likely to find them growing.

....

....

....

....

....

....

....

....

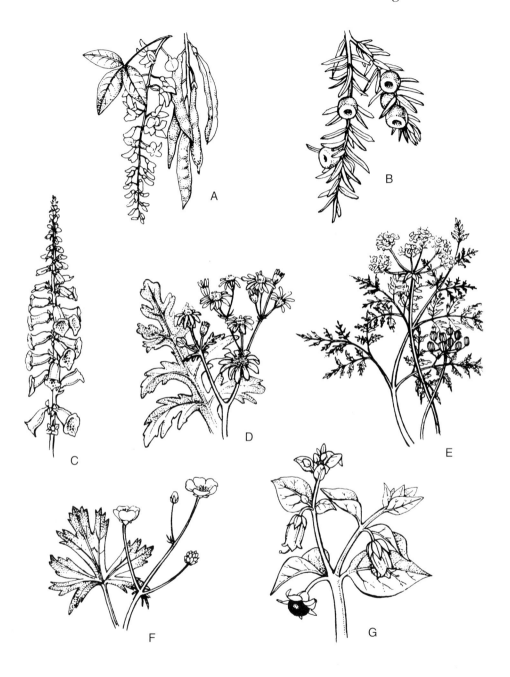

15. Explain how you maintain a horse paddock so that it remains a safe and healthy environment for horses.

   ....

   ....

   ....

   ....

16. What should you check in the horse's field every day?

   ....

   ....

   ....

17. How often should you check field-kept horses? Explain why.

   ....

   ....

   ....

18. How often should a field be rested? What does it depend upon?

   ....

   ....

   ....

   ....

   ....

19. How much room should horses have when they are kept at grass?

....

20. Why is it a good idea to collect horses' droppings from the field. How often should it be done?

....

....

....

12 Feeding and Watering

Questions

1. Why should horses be fed little and often?

   ....

   ....

   ....

2. Why should horses be fed only good quality feed?

   ....

   ....

   ....

3. Why should horses be fed at regular intervals?

   ....

   ....

   ....

4. Why should horses have a supply of fresh water accessible at all times?

   ....

   ....

   ....

5. There are several "feed according to" points, like "feed according to work being done". List and explain a further five points.

....

....

....

....

....

....

....

....

6. List and explain four more rules of feeding and watering.

....

....

....

....

....

....

....

....

7. Describe and explain the pros and cons of different watering systems in the field and in the stable.

....

....

....

....

....

....

....

....

8. How do you make a bran mash and what would you use it for?

....

....

....

9. How are sugar beet pulp and sugar beet cubes prepared?

....

....

....

....

....

10. In simple terms, explain the feed value of oats, barley, and sugar beet.

....

....

....

....

....

....

....

....

11. In simple terms, explain the feed value of bran.

....

....

....

....

12. What care must be taken when feeding different types of nuts and cubes?

....

....

....

13. Identify the six feeds pictured below. Start with the feed in the small bowl, then the larger bowl, and then work clockwise.

....

....

....

....

....

....

....

....

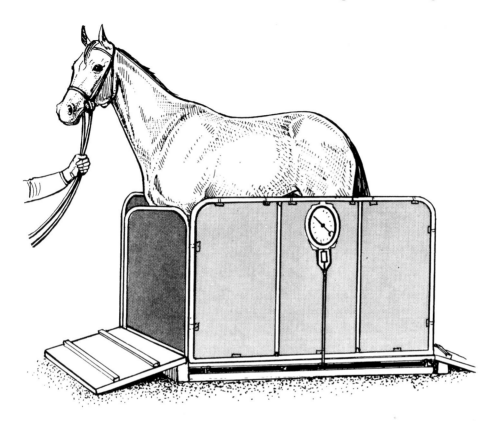

14. What is happening here? Explain why it is helpful to do this.

....

....

....

....

....

....

15. In simple terms, explain what coarse mixes are like and what feed value they have.

....

....

....

....

16. How do you calculate how much, and what, to feed your horse.

....

....

....

....

17. What would you feed to a sick or resting horse?

....

....

18. If your horse has a respiratory problem how can you help it through careful feeding?

....

....

....

....

19. How would the feed differ for a young horse in comparison to an old horse?

....

....

....

....

20. How does feeding differ for horses and ponies at grass in the summer and in the winter?

....

....

....

....

21. Why might you use a feed chart?

....

....

22. What would you write on a feed chart?

....

....

....

....

23. Why might you feed soaked hay to a horse?

....

....

....

24. How would you go about soaking the hay ready for feeding?

....

....

....

....

25. What other alternatives to soaked hay could be used? What are the pros and cons of each alternative?

....

....

....

....

....

....

....

....

26. Why might you feed "boiled barley" to a horse?

....

....

....

....

27. How is boiled barley prepared?

....

....

....

....

28. Explain how flaked and micronised barley differ from plain rolled barley.

....

....

....

....

....

....

13 Travelling

Questions

1. Where is the best place to position a horsebox or trailer ready for loading a horse?

   ....

   ....

   ....

   ....

2. If your horse is to be sent on a journey in a trailer or horsebox, what items of equipment could you use for the horse's comfort and protection?

   ....

   ....

   ....

   ....

   ....

   ....

3. What else might a horse wear for travelling?

   ....

   ....

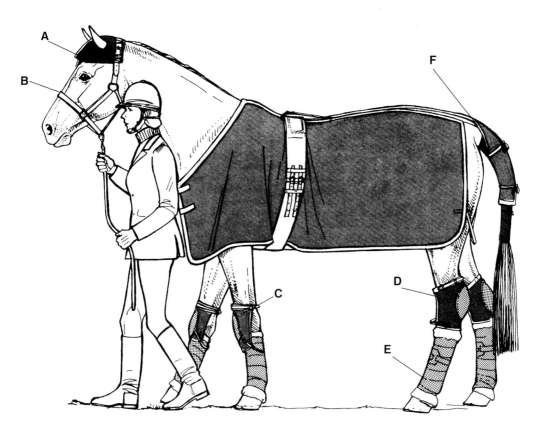

4. Name the items of equipment, A to F, worn by this horse. Explain the use of each item.

....

....

....

....

....

....

5. What is a poll guard and when would you use it?

....

....

6. When your horse is travelling, why should you use a leather headcollar?

....

....

....

....

7. What factors do you consider when deciding what rug, if any, to put on your horse for travelling?

....

....

....

....

8. Would you always put a tail bandage on your horse for travelling?

....

....

....

....

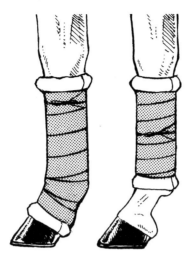

9. When travelling your horse, which of these two types of bandage would you use? Explain your choice.

   ....

   ....

   ....

   ....

   ....

   ....

10. What is a tail guard and when would you use it?

   ....

   ....

   ....

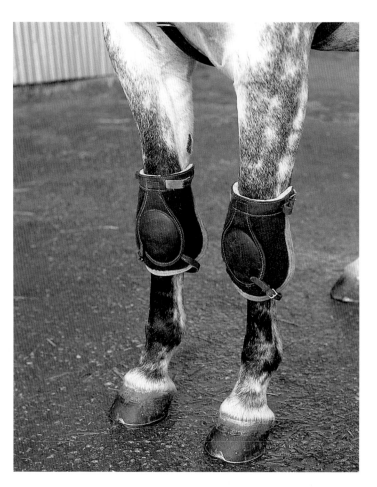

11. Identify the equipment fitted to this horse's legs.

....

12. What is the equipment used for? Describe how it is fitted.

....

....

....

13. What are hock boots for? How should they be fitted?

....

....

....

....

14. What can you use if you do not have knee and hock boots?

....

....

15. Is it best to travel a horse with a minimum amount of protective equipment fitted, or is it best to use everything available?

....

....

....

....

16. Give some good and bad points for using travelling boots and travelling bandages.

....

....

....

....

17. When travelling your horse, would you fit overreach boots? If so, why?

....

....

....

....

18. Is it necessary to familiarise a horse with travelling equipment before the journey? If so, how would you do this?

....

....

....

....

19. Should you clothe the horse ready for travelling just before or well in advance of the journey? Give reasons for your answer.

....

....

....

....

20. What should a handler wear when loading a horse?

....

....

21. Describe the procedure to adopt when leading a horse up and into a horsebox.

....

....

....

....

....

22. If a horse does not want to go into a horsebox what can be done to encourage it?

....

....

....

....

....

23. Describe the unloading procedure to adopt when taking a horse out of a trailer.

....

....

....

....

....

24. Describe the unloading procedure to adopt when taking a horse out of a horsebox.

....

....

....

....

....

25. What are the pros and cons of using a trailer in preference to a horsebox?

....

....

....

....

....

26. How is a horse most likely to be injured when being unloaded from a horsebox or trailer?

....

....

....

....

....

....

27. For what reasons might you check on a horse during a journey?

....

....

....

....

28. What particular care should the driver of a horsebox or trailer take during a journey?

....

....

....

....

14 Lungeing

Questions

1. Name the items of equipment, A to E, worn by the horse below. Explain the use of each item.

   ....

   ....

   ....

   ....

   ....

   ....

2. Why would you lunge a horse?

....

....

....

....

3. For how long would you lunge a horse and at what pace?

....

....

....

....

4. Explain the procedure for starting the horse off on the lunge circle.

....

....

....

5. What equipment should the person lungeing wear, and why?

....

....

....

....

6. Explain the technique the person lungeing the horse should adopt.

....

....

....

....

....

7. Should the horse always be fully tacked-up for lungeing? If not, why not?

....

....

....

....

....

8. Explain the safe procedure the person lungeing the horse should adopt, and the dangers to be aware of.

....

....

....

....

....

9. Is lungeing useful as part of a fitness programme? If so, why?

    ....

    ....

    ....

    ....

10. When lungeing for exercise what are the benefits of putting a saddle on the horse?

    ....

    ....

    ....

    ....

15 General Knowledge

Questions

1. When riding out in the countryside, what is considered the polite and courteous way of approaching other riders and countryside users?

   ....

   ....

   ....

   ....

   ....

2. List, and explain, four rules of country lore that should be observed when riding out in the countryside.

   ....

   ....

   ....

   ....

   ....

   ....

   ....

   ....

3. Explain three more points of recommended behaviour and safe procedure to adopt when riding out in the countryside.

....

....

....

....

4. List, and explain, some dos and don'ts for riding on the public roadways.

....

....

....

....

....

5. Outline the recommended procedure to adopt in the event of an accident.

....

....

....

....

....

....

6. What steps should be taken, in various situations, to ensure that further problems and/or injuries do not occur following an accident?

....

....

....

....

....

....

7. Under what circumstances might you put a person who has fallen off their horse into the recovery position?

....

....

....

....

....

....

8. Outline the structure of the British Horse Society (BHS).

....

....

....

9. What different subdivisions and committees make up the structure of the BHS?

    ....

    ....

    ....

    ....

10. What are the benefits of membership of the BHS?

    ....

    ....

    ....

    ....

Exam Notes

Apply to the examinations office of the British Horse Society for application forms, a syllabus and the current fees.

Examiners are human

1. The jobs they have

- The majority of examiners work within the horse industry; for example, full- or part-time at agricultural colleges as lecturers in equine studies, or maybe as a yard manager for the equine department at the college.
- Some examiners have their own equine businesses, which may involve livery, schooling, competing, and/or teaching.
- Other examiners may no longer work in the equine industry, but generally have maintained links with the horse world by owning their own horses and competing in their spare time.
- By means of such jobs and connections, examiners keep up-to-date and are aware of new trends and new ways considered acceptable for carrying out certain tasks. Therefore, candidates should not think that examiners are out of date, or out of touch with current trends.

2. Examiners go through the exam system too

- All examiners will have worked their way through the same examination system as that which candidates themselves are working through.
- Older examiners may well have qualified before more recent changes to the BHS examination system; nonetheless, they still have had to take the BHS examination to qualify.
- Having been through the exam system themselves (some of them very recently), examiners are well aware of how stressful exams can be and know what candidates are going through.

- Individual candidates may have to go through the process of having to re-take an examination. Likewise, some examiners themselves may have been unsuccessful and therefore will have gone through this experience too.

3. *Examiner training*

- All examiners have to attend regular examiner training days to be eligible to continue as an examiner.
- These training days take different forms. At regional level, for example, examiners often take turns in role play. Here, one examiner is the candidate and one is the examiner and another is an observer. In this way, each examiner can experience the taking of an examination from each different person's point of view.
- National examiner training days often take the form of lecture demonstrations and question and answer sessions. This gives examiners a chance to share ideas and learn new techniques.
- Examiner training puts examiners in a similar position to candidates. They experience being asked questions and have to carry out tasks under scrutiny.
- So, candidates should understand that examiners really do know how those being tested are feeling on the day, as they will have been through a similar situation, quite recently, themselves.
- Examiners also have to hold a current First Aid certificate to meet health and safety requirements. The certificate only lasts for three years at a time. Thereafter, examiners must attend a refresher course and sit the First Aid examination every three years.
- Once again, examiners experience first hand the exam situation as a candidate themselves. So they know how you are feeling.

4. *They want to pass you*

- There is nothing more pleasant for examiners than being able to pass all the candidates at an exam day.
- For examiners, the day passes quickly and easily if the candidates are well prepared and up to standard.
- It is hard work trying to gain information from a candidate who is struggling with the tasks and questions.

- Examiners will "feel" the stress of a candidate who is not coping and this makes for an uncomfortable and sometimes worrying exam session.
- Candidates who are unsuccessful are given brief written reports, which outline where they made mistakes in the exam. This is all more work for examiners and makes for a long day.
- There is nothing better than a day when everyone passes.

5. *The role of the Chief Examiner*

- The Chief Examiner is an experienced examiner whose task it is to oversee the entire exam day. He or she will endeavour to see a small piece of work in every section of the exam, in order to gain an overview of the abilities of each candidate.
- Before the exam day, the Chief Examiner will have received a list of candidates and a list of the examiners who will make up the examining team for the day.
- The Chief Examiner will contact each member of the exam team, and let them know which section of the exam they are to examine. In this way each examiner can be prepared for their section.
- The Chief Examiner will also contact the examination centre and discuss the plan for the day and agree on the format to follow.
- On the day, the Chief Examiner will meet up with the examining team and make sure everyone is prepared. He or she will then introduce themselves and the examining team to the candidates and make sure that all those taking the exam have arrived.
- A number is allocated to each candidate. This helps the exam team identify each candidate without mistakes. At this stage, also, candidates are provided with a programme for the day so that they all know where they are supposed to be and when.
- Throughout the day the Chief Examiner will "float", moving from one section to another, keeping an eye on the time, and prompting examiners to bring their section to a conclusion if necessary.
- The Chief Examiner will endeavour to take down results from each examiner as each section is completed, in order to keep track of the day's progress.
- At the end of the day, the Chief Examiner compiles results with

the aid of the exam team, fills in the official results sheet (which will be returned to the examinations office), and prepares to give candidates their results.

- Each Chief Examiner will have their own way of giving the results. Some read straight down their list, giving results in candidate number order. Some will take the unsuccessful candidates to one side for their results, and others will give each candidate their results individually.
- Once the results have been announced, the examining team will debrief any of the candidates who request a first-hand report on their performance during the day. The Chief Examiner will listen to these debriefings.
- It is a good idea for candidates to take notes at this point, as it is so easy to forget what has been said at the end of a tiring day.
- Finally, the Chief Examiner will debrief any of the examiners as he or she thinks necessary and then say a thank you for the day to the host at the examination centre before leaving. On return home, or as soon as possible, the Chief Examiner posts examination results and copies of any report forms that were filled in to the examinations office of the BHS where the official results are recorded.

6. Candidate preparation

- When taking the first three stages of the BHS examinations, candidates can take the exams at the same centre at which they have trained. Some candidates will train at a centre, then take the exam elsewhere. There can be advantages and disadvantages to both.
- Training, then taking the exam at the same centre helps the candidate to feel "at home" and relaxed. He or she will know their way around, and know the horses they are working with. They will be familiar with the yard staff and able to ask for help easily, and will usually have their equipment to hand. For example, it is unlikely that they will find they have left their hat or boots at home.
- However, it is easy to be "sloppy" when working in familiar surroundings and with familiar horses. This can lead to mistakes and make a poor impression.

- Candidates taking the exam at an unfamiliar centre are more likely to be on their best behaviour, treating all horses with caution and being more particular about tasks when using unfamiliar equipment.
- However, they have the disadvantage of not knowing their way around and may find it more difficult to relax amongst people they do not know.
- It is essential that all candidates read the exam syllabus. When taking the exam, you must feel confident, in your own mind, that you have covered every single item on the syllabus and that you fully understand it.
- Each individual must be responsible for their own training. Too many candidates rely totally on their trainers to make sure they have covered all the necessary subjects. If you missed a lecture, one day, for whatever reason, it is not up to the trainer to make sure you cover the missed subject. It is up to you. You must take responsibility for your own training.
- Take great care to make sure that you have the correct clothing and equipment for the day. It is quite a good idea to have a dress rehearsal. If you try out your intended exam clothing, you can check that you will be comfortable riding or working in it, and you can ask an experienced person for their opinion on how you look.
- The fit and cut of a hacking jacket can make a big difference to the way you look on a horse. Your choice of working clothing can make a big difference to your performance and comfort and the impression you make.
- Always check details regarding certificates and documents that you may need to have with you on exam day. Sometimes, for example, it is necessary to show a Riding and Road Safety Certificate; you may not be allowed to complete the exam if you don't have it with you. So, check these details well in advance.
- If you are going to an unfamiliar centre to take the exam, make sure that you visit it in advance. By doing this you can check the route and how long it takes to get there. On arrival, introduce yourself and ask if you can have a look round. Most centres are always happy to show you around so that you can familiarise

yourself with the layout. In this way you will feel more confident on the day.

- Sometimes it is helpful to have a doctor's note if you have a condition that examiners should know about. For example, if you are asthmatic and need an inhaler, examiners would rather know about it, then they can allow you to use your inhaler as necessary.

- However, it is not a good idea to bring a doctor's certificate which says that you have a hip/leg/arm, etc., injury. Whilst examiners will take into consideration problems like ongoing chronic conditions, if you are not fit to take the exam, you should not be there at all.

7. *Coping with the day*

- Always plan to arrive early. This will give you time to find your way around the centre. For example, you need to locate the reception area, and the toilets.

- If you are taking a riding exam, the jumping course will be laid out ready, and candidates are encouraged to walk the course at the start of the day.

- Some centres have refreshment facilities, or you may bring refreshments with you. Take time to sit and relax and have something to drink while you compose yourself.

- It is always a good idea to have someone accompany you to the exam. Having someone to talk to, who can also take care of your belongings during the day, and perhaps be ready with a change of coat, etc., as necessary, is reassuring specially at an unfamiliar centre.

- Another good idea is to have someone drive you to and from the exam. A candidate who is nervous with anticipation of the exam day, and then afterwards may be tired, elated, or disappointed, is not in the best frame of mind to concentrate on driving.

- Make sure you take all the equipment you will need. For example, hat, boots, gloves, hairnet, jacket, pens, any certificates required, are all easily forgotten. Take different coats for changing weather and any other spare items you may like to have with you just in case.

- Be friendly towards the other candidates. You may find it reassuring to find that they are just as nervous as you are, but don't let another candidate make you feel more nervous. Occasionally you may come across a candidate who feels the need to show off how much knowledge and experience they have. This may leave you feeling inadequately prepared, if you take too much notice. However, you will probably discover that they know no more than you; they just feel the need to show off as it makes them feel more confident, when underneath they are really very nervous.

- During the course of the day, you will be examined in groups of four or five – or maybe more, depending upon the total number of candidates. At Stage One, there can be up to 18 candidates taking the exam.

- Each group session will last threequarters of an hour to one hour.

- The Stage Two exam is completed in one day, starting at 9.00 a.m. and finishing for lunch at 1.15 p.m. approximately. The restart will be at 3.00 p.m. approximately, to finish at 4.00 p.m. There will be five group sessions: Riding (including jumping), Practical, Practical/Oral, Theory, and Lungeing.

- There are no written papers at Stage Two. All question and answer sessions are verbal or practical demonstrations.

- Make sure you have made arrangements for lunch. It is best to bring sandwiches with you, as this is quick and easy. Going to a local pub can take too much time, and you may find yourself missing out because you don't manage to get served on time. Lunch breaks are usually short, and examiners do not expect to wait for anyone.

- After a long car journey, and especially on a cold day, you may find yourself quite stiff, and likely to be a little rigid. If you are scheduled to ride first thing, try some loosening up exercises before you start – perhaps a quick run around the indoor school!

- It is important that you take the day seriously. However, this doesn't mean going around with a grim expression on your face. Try to keep smiling, and keep up a professional and friendly approach. Most people have a favourable impression of someone who presents themselves in this way.

- Most important of all, is not to take the exam before you are ready. You really need to be above standard to allow for nerves making you perform below your normal level on the day. If you are only just up to standard, then on the day you are bound to fall below standard. So, don't try to rush your exams; be patient, and avoid disappointment.

8. *Examiner's expectations and what they would like to see*

- Examiners are well aware that candidates are likely to be nervous, especially at the beginning of the day. They hope that candidates will gradually settle and gain confidence as the day progresses. They will make allowances for nerves; for example, it is quite likely that some candidates will become flustered, or go to do something one way and then change their mind. Examiners will put this down to nerves and will not think badly of candidates if this happens. So, don't let your nervous feelings worry you too much.
- As candidates progress through the levels in their training, examiners will expect them to appear more confident at the corresponding exams. Examiners will, however, still allow for a degree of nervousness at the beginning of any examination.
- One of the best ways for a candidate to make a good impression, is to be enthusiastic. Candidates who stand around looking bored will not do themselves any favours. Candidates should show a keenness to carry out tasks and answer questions.
- It is important that candidates do remember that these exams are intended for professionals. Each exam stage leads towards qualifications that can result in the candidate becoming an instructor or manager in charge. It is therefore advantageous to project yourself as a mature person. For example, when talking about daily grazing management, DON'T say "poos" and DO say "droppings" need to be picked up. Think before you speak and project your mature approach by using the correct terminology.
- Throughout the day, you need to relate to the examiners and the other candidates in a positive and friendly way. Treat examiners with respect. Whether you know them or not, you should not be on Christian name terms during the exam. Give them space to make notes and to discuss points with their fellow examiners in

private. At the same time, be friendly and willing to talk to them should they invite you to make conversation.

- Try to be helpful to other candidates. Don't butt in when they are trying to answer a question, but do help out – if they are struggling to find a hoof pick for example. Try not to disagree with other people; this can be unnerving for the person you disagree with. Just state your opinion. For example, you may say "I would do it this way."

- Throughout the exam, the examiners will need to spread their time amongst the candidates. When another candidate is being asked a question, or asked to perform a particular task, continue to remain aware and involved.

- For example, if a candidate is asked to trot up a horse, watch and listen. Show that you are interested. Examiners will be watching you all the time and not just when you are asked to do something specific. How you behave throughout the day will help to create an impression on the examiners.

- If the examiner says you have completed a section and that you can go on to the next, remember your training. The examiner will notice the candidate who checks that equipment has been put away tidily, that the stable door is properly bolted, and that the horse has been left secure and comfortable in its stable. So, you must be thinking all the time; it is tiring, but you are under scrutiny all through the day.

- Examiners know that mistakes are made. They do not expect candidates to go through the whole day without a single mistake. So don't panic if you think you have done something wrong. Approach the examiner and tell him or her what it is you are concerned about, and how you would like to put it right.

9. *Exam technique*

- The exam day will be tiring, but it is very important to remain alert throughout. Be aware of what is going on around you. Listen to others, and keep track of what is happening so that you can contribute at the right time. For example, another candidate may be loading a horse into a horse box, and you may notice a wheelbarrow in the way. If you are alert you will be able to step forward and help – showing that you are aware and able when needed.

- Be tactful towards other candidates. If you think another person has answered a question incorrectly, rather than saying you disagree, or that they are wrong, simply say, for example, "I would do it this way, ..." or "In my opinion, . . . "
- Try to put yourself forward whenever there is an opportunity to do so – but not too often. If you keep on coming forward with answers, examiners will tend to give others a chance. Whereas, if you always wait to be asked for an answer, examiners will tend to keep asking you questions to find out what you know. So be forward, without being pushy.
- Make sure you use the correct technical terms whenever appropriate. This gives a professional and knowledgeable impression.
- During the day you will give a good impression if you move quickly from one place to another. As candidates finish one section, and move on to another part of the stable yard, they should aim to do so as quickly as possible. If you need a drink or a toilet break, then let the examiner know, so they're not searching for you.
- Do ask questions when necessary. If an examiner asks you to do something, or phrases a question in such a way that you don't understand what is wanted, don't be afraid to ask for clarification. All examiners know that sometimes they may be misunderstood, and are experienced in rephrasing themselves to aid understanding. Whatever you do, don't try to carry on without being completely clear about the task or question.
- Follow these guidelines and you should sail through! Good luck.

10. End of day discussions

- When the examination is over, the examiners will gather together and compare notes and compile results.
- If any reports need to be written, this will be done now.
- Each examiner will give their final results to the Chief Examiner. He or she will then check that all is accounted for and prepare to read out the exam results to the candidates.

- At this point certificates are filled in for successful candidates, and all the paperwork is completed. This can take some time.
- If there has been an accident during the day, an accident report must be filled in with all the relevant information.
- If a candidate is considered to be borderline in any part of the exam, examiners will discuss the candidate's performance and try to come to a conclusion on whether or not he or she is to be given a pass or be deemed unsuccessful. Every effort is made to highlight the candidate's positive points to see if they outweigh the negative. These discussions can take some time, and examiners will never hurry their results.
- Candidates should not worry if examiners seem to disappear for a long time. The examination team need to make sure that there are no mistakes and will not rush their discussions. They will, however, complete their task as quickly as possible and different groups work at different rates. Much will depend on the number of candidates.

Good luck on the day.

Answers to the Questions

1. A. Leather wisp. B. Grooming mitts. C. Grooming machines.
2. A wisp is a pad made from hay, or leather filled with stuffing.
3. A wisp is used for helping to tone up the horse's muscles, particularly over its hindquarters.
4. Some people refer to wisping as "banging" or "strapping".
5. Strapping is the full and thorough grooming process as applied to a fit, stable-kept horse and it includes some wisping.
6. Rather than making wisps from hay, it is now possible to buy a leather pad. The latter is usually of a circular or oval shape and has a loop for the hand so it is easy to hold and use.
7. Start with the hoof pick and pick out the feet. Next, use a rubber curry comb to bring the grease and dirt to the surface all over the horse's body. Then use a body brush, to groom the mane and forelock. Continue with the body brush and curry comb and work over the whole of the horse's body. Start at the head, then work down the neck, shoulder, front leg, along the back and barrel, over the hindquarters and down the hind limb. Repeat on the other side of the horse. Then groom the tail using the body brush and your fingers. Finish off by sponging the eyes, nose, and under the tail. Then give the horse a final dust over with a stable rubber.
8. When wisping, the aim is to make the horse's muscles tense and relax, so helping them to develop and become stronger. The wisp is held in one hand and a stable rubber in the other. The groom should raise his or her arm when using the wisp, so that the horse can see it, and then bring the wisp down with a light bang on to an area of muscle. This action is followed by a stroke over the same muscle area using the stable rubber to relax the muscles. This process is repeated many times, depending on how fit the horse is. Once into a routine and a rhythm, the horse will tense its muscles ready for the wisp each time. The wisp should be brought down firmly enough to make the horse tense its muscles, but not so firmly that it would cause pain.

9. Horses in hard work – eventing, racing, showjumping, and the higher levels of dressage are examples – would benefit from being wisped.

10. Sometimes an injured horse may benefit from being wisped if it has some muscle wastage and needs help with building up the muscles again.

11. Quartering is the process of grooming the horse in four stages, each quarter at a time.

12. When a stable-kept horse is rugged up in the winter, a quick tidy up, before morning exercise, can be carried out. By folding back the rug, one quarter at a time, each quarter of the horse can be groomed without the horse getting cold.

13. Horses are groomed to improve their appearance, to prevent disease, and to promote good health. Grooming is also a time for the handler to build a relationship with the horse, whilst getting to know every inch of its body. By keeping the horse clean, the risk of disease is minimised, there are no hidden wounds, sores, or places where infection may set in and where mites or lice may take up residence. The grooming process also helps to release natural, protective oils into the horse's coat and stimulates circulation, so aiding good health. By getting to know the horse really well, the handler will quickly notice if a lump, area of heat, or anything unusual should appear. Action can then be taken to solve a minor problem before it becomes a big problem.

14. (i)   First, make sure that the horse is cool and dry and that it's breathing rate has returned to normal. To do this, remove the tack and walk the horse quietly in hand. In cold weather, put a light rug on the horse to keep it warm. In warm weather, the horse could be washed down to remove sweat and mud; whilst doing this, the horse should be checked carefully, all over, to make sure that no injuries have been sustained. The horse should also be offered a drink, but only a small amount at approximately two minute intervals until it has quenched its thirst. Pick out the horse's feet and check its shoes. Leave the horse to rest in a warm, dry stable with plenty of bedding. In the summer, the horse could be turned out in a small paddock to rest, as long as it can be easily checked.

(ii)   Having made sure that the horse has not sustained any injuries, be careful to check that its behaviour is normal and that it gives no signs of colic or general distress. The horse's legs should be checked several times, as heat and swelling may appear after the general recovery period.

(iii)   During cold weather, clean water that has been slightly warmed should be offered to the horse. Allow the horse to drink a small amount at a time and keep offering the water approximately every two minutes until the horse does not appear to want any more. Then leave the horse with a bucket of water in its stable.

(iv)   In the summer, the horse can be given cold water straight from the tap as long as, to begin with, only a small amount is given at a time. In cold winter weather conditions, the water should be slightly warmed by the addition of hot water just to take the chill off.

(v)   Check those areas of the horse's skin where the saddle and bridle sit. Look for rubs and sores, in case sweat or dirt has gathered and caused friction or injury. The legs should be checked for cuts, scratches, knocks, and brushing wounds; the heels for over-reach wounds, and the limbs for heat and swelling once the horse has had time to cool down.

(vi)   The horse's feet should be checked to make sure that no stones are lodged there. Also check that the shoes are all still in place, secure and not twisted or loose.

Chapter 2: **Tack and Clothing**

1. Most horse turnout rugs have leg straps. They are passed between the horse's hind legs, linked together and then clipped on to the two back corners of the rug. Some designs have straps, called a "spider", which clips on to the front breast section of the rug, then passes between the front legs and divides into two branches. Each branch passes through a ring on the side of the rug, then between the hind legs and on to a ring at the back corner of the rug. Others have cross surcingles and most have double breast straps.

2. The roller being worn in this picture is an anti-cast roller.

3. An anti-cast roller is used if a stabled horse has a tendency to get cast. Some horses stabled in a stable which is slightly too small

for them, may be more likely to get cast and this type of roller may help in preventing this.

4. If a horse finds its rug too hot or uncomfortable in some way, it may try to remove the rug by biting and tearing at it. Some horses are quite successful at removing their rugs, depending on the design.

5. When horses are wet after having a bath, or sweaty after work, they could catch a chill while drying. Rugs that wick away moisture help to dry horses and keep them warm at the same time. This is especially helpful in cold weather and after exercise.

6. Rugs should be washed as soon as the lining gets dirty, which may be once a week or once a month. Some modern rugs can be washed in a conventional washing machine, but others need to go to a specialist cleaner.

7. Turnout rugs often have a waterproof coating. This is best just brushed with a stiff brush. The lining of the rug can be scrubbed with soap and water, rinsed – perhaps using a hosepipe – and then be hung out to dry.

8. Rugs which are not to be used for any length of time should be stored in a warm, dry area. They should also be hung up; this prevents creasing and future leaks in turnout rugs. When stored away rugs may be damaged by moths and vermin so preventive steps should be taken.

9. When bandaging for warmth and protection, stable bandages with gamgee or fybagee underneath should be used. The bandages should be applied from just below the knee, right the way down over the fetlock joint and pastern. Take care to apply the bandages with an even tension all the way. Allow some of the gamgee/fybagee to extend above and below the bandages so that the knees and the coronet bands are also protected as well.

10. The gamgee/fybagee is used under the bandages to help to distribute the pressure of the bandage and prevent pressure ridges at each turn.

11. Thick, fluffy, bandages, usually called "polo bandages" can be applied without padding underneath. The thickness of the bandage serves as built-in padding. At the same time, the bandages are not stretchy, so they cannot be applied too tightly.

12. Bandages can help to keep a tired horse warm. Similarly, a horse

which has become unwell, especially in the winter and if it has been clipped, will benefit from bandaging. Keeping the horse's extremeties warm means that it is less likely to require heavy layers of rugs; when a horse has had a strenuous day or is weak through ill health it may well find rugs tiring.

13. There is a possibility of injury when horses are loaded and unloaded into a trailer or horsebox and travelled. Bandages can protect the vulnerable parts of horses' legs, especially during the journey. Horses can also be bandaged for protection when they are exercised.

14. Overreach boots.

15. Overreach boots are bell-shaped rubber boots worn over the horse's hoof. They protect the heel and the coronet band.

16. Overreach boots are sometimes called "bell boots".

17. If a horse has a small injury on the heel or coronet area of its hind foot, an overreach boot might be worn to protect the area from knocks while the horse is working.

18. If the overreach boot is too small, or badly fitted, it may cause rubbing around the pastern where the neck of the boot sits.

19. A. Simple brushing boots. B. Open-fronted tendon boots. C. Brushing boots with extra tendon support and fetlock protection.

20. The pull-on style is the most simple, but can be quite difficult to put on and take off. The type with Velcro fastenings is simple to put on, but the Velcro can lose its grip and fail to secure the boot. A good idea is the type made with a plastic strip which links the two ends of the boot together; it makes a secure fastening, is fairly easy to fit, and replacement straps can be purchased. There is also a "petal" design where the boot is made up of a number of different sections threaded onto a strap which buckles around the pastern.

21. When horses are being lunged, they can easily lose balance and knock themselves. Simple brushing boots give adequate protection in such a situation. Any young horse may be unbalanced and simple brushing boots help to protect their limbs. When a boisterous horse is turned out in the field for a short period, simple brushing boots will protect it from knocks as it "lets off steam".

22. It is better not to fit boots to a horse for hunting or for a very long

ride over varying terrain and through mud and water. Mud and grit can get trapped under the boots and if the boots are on the horse's limbs for long periods rubbing will occur. This will cause the horse harm rather than provide protection.

23. Ill-fitting brushing boots can rub at the back of the knee or front of the hock or they may rub the heels or leave pressure ridges where straps are tight directly against a limb.

24. The width of the saddle tree, where it fits over the horse's withers, is the part of the saddle that is "narrow", "medium", or "wide".

25. The withers and the top of the shoulders are directly affected by the width of the saddle.

26. Saddles are measured from the stud at the side and front of the pommel in a straight line to the centre of the cantle.

27. Most adults would use a 17–18 in saddle.

28. To fit a saddle, select the width of the saddle you think most appropriate for your horse. Place it on the horse's back. There should be a good 10 cm (4 in) clearance over the horse's withers and a clear space along the whole length of the spine. The panels of the saddle should be in contact with the horse's back, to spread the rider's weight evenly. The saddle flaps and knee rolls should not interfere with the shoulders. Girth up the saddle and, if all appears to fit well, sit on the saddle to make sure that it remains a good fit.

29. The weight of the rider will effect the fit of the saddle, so the saddle must be checked with the rider seated. The rider, too, needs to check that the saddle is comfortable and the right size.

30. Ill-fitting saddles may rub on the horse's withers and back and either side of the spine.

31. Bridles are purchased in "pony", "cob", and "full" sizes.

32. Assemble the bridle and bit, then hold it up to the horse's head to get an approximate idea of the necessary adjustment. Then slip it on to the horse's head and check that the bit is sitting so it just wrinkles the corners of the horse's mouth. Make sure that the browband holds the headpiece just behind the ears, without pulling it forward, and that it is not too tight. Adjust a cavesson noseband to sit with room for two fingers between the front of the nose and the noseband itself. Adjust the noseband to sit the width of two fingers below the projecting cheekbones.

33. A poor-fitting bridle may rub behind the horse's ears, make the corners of the mouth sore, and rub sores where the noseband sits.

34. To lunge a horse for exercise, the saddle and bridle are optional. The lunge cavesson and lunge line are needed, along with side reins. Brushing boots on all four legs are advisable. A lungeing roller is needed if a saddle is not used.

35. In the illustration, the horse is wearing a bridle with a lunge cavesson and lunge line attached to the central nose ring of the cavesson.

36. When being lunged, horses often lose their balance, become boisterous and behave in an excitable manner. This can result in a horse knocking itself so brushing boots should be fitted as a precaution.

37. Using a saddle for lungeing exercise provides a point of contact for the side reins and can help to firm up the horse's saddle area for ridden work. Also, the horse can be ridden immediately after lungeing. However, if the horse is not to be ridden or if it has a bad back or has not yet worn a saddle, it is better and quicker to fit a lungeing roller before the exercise starts.

38. Place the bridle on the horse's head, first. Then fit the cavesson over the top. If you then decide to ride the horse after lungeing, you can easily slip off the lunge cavesson. The nose strap and jowl strap of the lunge cavesson should be fitted underneath the bridle cheekpieces so that they do not interfere with the position of the bit.

39. The side reins should be attached to the girth straps of the saddle. Pass the side rein underneath the first girth strap, then thread the second strap through the side rein. This makes for a secure attachment. Make sure that the side reins are above the buckle guard.

40. Adjust the side reins so that they reach the bit when the horse is holding its head in a normal, relaxed walking position.

41. The lunge line should be attached to the centre ring on the cavesson.

42. The girth straps, stirrup leathers and girth should be checked for signs of wear. If the stitching is starting to rot, any of these parts could snap very easily. The reins should be carefully checked on the bridle: should they break the rider will have no control.

Straps on boots must be checked for signs of wear, to avoid them snapping when in use. A general check of the stitching and strength of the leather on all accessories is advisable.

43. A martingale or breastplate can help to stop a saddle from slipping back. If the horse's saddle is inclined to slip during lungeing, these items can help to secure the saddle. And if a horse is normally ridden in a martingale, it will be easier for the person lungeing to have the horse tacked up in its normal riding equipment should he or she intend to ride the horse immediately after lungeing.

44. The martingale has a neck strap which would sit easily around the base of the neck, being neither tight or very loose. The strap which runs from the girth, should follow the contours of the underline of the horse's neck. Where the strap divides into two with rings that slip onto each rein, it should appear loose when the horse is at rest and come into action when the rider has a rein contact and the horse tries to raise its head above the point of control.

45. The wither strap on the breastplate should lie over the horse's withers with room for the rider's hands to fit between withers and and strap. The two little straps that buckle on to the saddle should be adjusted so they hold the breastplate firmly in place. The two straps that sit either side of the neck should meet at the base of the neck without being tight or loose. The single strap that then passes between the front legs and on to the girth should just sit about 2.5 cm (1 in) clear of the horse's chest so it is neither tight or loose.

46. Fetlock boots can be made of leather or man-made synthetic material. They will be secured with a buckle or Velcro fastening. Brushing boots may be made of leather or synthetic material and are usually secured with straps and buckles or Velcro. Tendon boots are also made of leather or synthetic material. Most are secured with straps or buckles.

47. Fetlock boots are used if a horse is inclined to knock itself in the fetlock area, thus causing bruising and damage. The fetlock boots can protect the horse from damaging itself. Brushing boots are worn if a horse is inclined to knock itself anywhere on its lower limb. This often happens with young horses as they can be

unbalanced while learning; brushing boots protect them from minor knocks. Tendon boots are worn to help support and protect the tendons if the horse is doing more strenuous work, like jumping.

48. Any boots worn should be checked carefully to make sure they are clean when they are put on the horse. Even a small piece of grit can cause a great deal of damage to the horse if it rubs against the skin under the boot. The fit of boots should be carefully checked to make sure that they will not rub the horse when any of the joints of the lower limb are flexed, as this would also cause rubbing and sores.

49. A bit should sit across the width of the horse's mouth with no excess mouthpiece protruding on either side. The mouthpiece should be wide enough to sit comfortably without the horse's lips being pinched in by the bit rings. If the bit is too wide, it will slide around in the horse's mouth.

50. The thicker the mouthpiece of the bit, the milder the action. Pressure is spread over a greater area. The more narrow the mouthpiece, the more severe the bit, as pressure is concentrated on a smaller area.

51. When the horse is being ridden, the bit may apply pressure on the tongue, to the corners of the mouth, on the bars of the mouth, on the nose, and to the poll, depending on the type of bit.

52. Top: a loose ring, French snaffle. Bottom: a Pelham.

53. The five families are: snaffle; double bridle; Pelham; Gag; and bitless bridle.

Chapter 3: **The Foot and Shoeing**

1. Buffer, pincers, rasp, driving hammer, and drawing knife.
2. To remove the old shoes, the farrier will use the buffer, hammer, and pincers.
3. The farrier will knock up the clenches with the hammer and buffer, then lever off the shoe with the pincers.
4. To work on a front foot, farriers will usually bring the horse's foot between their own legs and hold it with their knees, leaving their hands free. For different parts of the shoeing process, farriers also use a tripod to support the foot.

5. A horse's hind foot can be supported on the farrier's thigh, by bringing the leg up and forward and then hooking it over the thigh just above the knee.

6. The farrier is resting the horse's hoof on a tripod while he uses the rasp to finish off and tidy up the foot having put on a new shoe.

7. A tripod is used for supporting any one of the horse's feet while the farrier finishes off the shoeing process with the rasp.

8. The rasp is used to help create a level bearing surface, ready for the shoe to be nailed on to the foot and to help finish off the process when the shoe has been nailed on.

9. The drawing knife is used for trimming the foot, for making a place for the toe clip, and for pairing away foot to expose a bruise or infected area within the foot. It may also be used for cutting off ragged portions of the frog.

10. Hoof cutters are used for cutting off large amounts of the wall of the foot, when it is long and overgrown.

11. Most horses have four nails on the outside branch of the shoe and three nails on the inside. For very small ponies, less nails may be used.

12. The clenching tongs are used to tighten down the clenches that keep the shoe in place.

13. The buffer is used for levering up the clenches prior to the shoe being removed.

14. Most horses need to be shod every four to six weeks.

15. Horses that do a great deal of road work will wear their shoes down very quickly. They need to be shod more often therefore. Some horses have weak, or problem feet which need more frequent attention from the farrier. In the spring, the feet of a horse living out at grass may grow more rapidly and need more frequent attention. Horses in light work, with good feet, will need less frequent visits from the farrier, but must not be left for very long periods.

16. Shoes left on too long are likely to start to bring pressure to bear on the seat of corn and cause bruising and lameness. Also, the angle of the foot will change and put unnecessary stress on other parts of the limb.

17. The horse's foot supports the horse and protects the end of the

limbs, it absorbs concussion and helps, as the horse moves, to pump blood back up the limbs.

18. As more is asked from horses than nature intended, they need shoes to protect their feet from excessive wear and to provide grip.
19. A. Coronet band. B. Wall. C. Toe. D. Periople. E. Heel. F. Quarter. G. Cleft of frog. H. Seat of corn. I. Bars. J. frog. K. Sole. L. White line. M. Wall. N. Bulbs of heel. O. End of long pastern. P. Short pastern. Q. Navicular bone. R. Deep digital flexor tendon. S. Plantar cushion. T. Frog. U. Sole. V. White line. W. Sensitive laminae. X. Pedal bone. Short pastern. Q. Navicular bone. R. Deep digital flexor tendon. S. Plantar cushion. T. Frog. U. Sole. V. White line. W. Sensitive laminae. X. Pedal bone. Y. Wall. Z. Common digital extensor tendon.
20. Take the hammer, buffer, and pincers. Lift a front foot and bring it between your knees to hold it, or rest a hind foot on your thigh just above your knee. Knock up the clenches by placing the buffer under each clench and knock it with the hammer. Take the pincers and lever off the shoe starting at the heels and levering forwards and inwards so as not to break the foot.

Chapter 4: **Stable Design**

1. For a 14hh pony, a stable approximately 300 cm x 300 cm (10 ft x 10 ft) should be of ample size.
2. For a 16hh horse a stable of between 360 cm x 360 cm (12 ft x 12 ft) and 420 cm x 420 cm (14 ft x 14 ft) is of ample size.
3. For an in-foal mare, a stable approximately 480 cm x 480 cm (16 ft x 16 ft) should be of ample size.
4. It is best to keep fittings and fixtures to a minimum in the stable, a tie-up ring being essential.
5. By keeping fittings and fixtures to a minimum you reduce the likelihood of the horse getting injured or caught up in its box.
6. Good features are: strong hinges, hooks to secure the door with when open, an anti-escape bolt on the bottom door, and an anti-chew strip along the top of the bottom door.
7. It is best to position the tie-up ring near the front of the box close

to the door, so that when you enter the box the horse is tied up with its head towards you.

8. When choosing a location for a stable consider the following: Is there easy access to power and water? Are there any large trees that may be a risk if they fall or their branches break off? Is the site well drained? Is the area generally accessible?

9. Stable floors are usually concrete. They should be slightly roughened, not completely smooth, so that they provide grip and will not be slippery. There should also be a slight slope for drainage purposes.

10. Slate provides good insulation and an attractive roof, but can easily break, and it is not always easily available. Roofing tiles are ideal, offering good insulation and being smart, but they are expensive. Corrugated iron is not a good material to use, as it offers poor insulation, can be noisy, and rusts easily. However, it is sometimes used as it is fairly cheap.

11. A stable door should be at least 2.5 m (8 ft) high and 1.25 m (4 ft) wide.

12. Horses can raise their heads very high. When startled, they are inclined to throw up their heads. If the roof is too low and they hit their head it could cause serious injury and will make the horse mistrust its stable environment. By using A-line roofs, plenty of headroom can be provided.

Chapter 5: **Clipping and Trimming**

1. Horses are clipped to improve their appearance, to enable them to work hard without getting very hot and stressed in the winter, and to help make keeping them clean easier, which in turn will help promote health and avoid disease.

2. If a horse has never been clipped, it is helpful to stand it near to an experienced horse while it is being clipped. In this way if can get used to the sound and see that the other horse is not afraid. Switch off the clippers and show them to the horse and run them over its coat. Then, standing near the horse's shoulder, switch the clippers on and gently begin clipping.

3. To help keep the mane and tail out of the way when clipping, put

on a tail bandage and plait the mane before starting to clip. The horse should be thoroughly groomed. The clippers will run through the coat more easily if the horse has been wearing a rug for some time.

4. The different types of clip are: A = Trace clip; B = Blanket clip; C = Chaser clip; D = Belly and neck clip; E = Hunter clip.

5. The area used for clipping should be undercover, dry, and well lit. Rubber matting, on the floor, is helpful and there must be a suitable power point.

6. The person clipping will need overalls and long hair is best tied back and covered with a hat or scarf. It is useful to have an assistant when clipping a horse. A mask may be needed, too, as a great deal of horse hair will be drifting around.

7. The clippers should have been well cleaned after the last clip. Check the cable and make sure that it is complete with no cracks. Sharp blades should be put onto the machine and be well oiled. Make sure that the air vents on the machine are clear.

8. To complete a hunter clip on a well-behaved horse will take an experienced person approximately 45 minutes to one hour.

9. During the clip, the blades should be checked frequently to make sure that they are not too hot. Cooling sprays can be applied to help in this. Hair which accumulates should be brushed away as often as necessary. Check that the air vents are clear and ensure that oil is applied to keep the blades and machine running smoothly.

10. A newly-sharpened set of blades will probably complete two blanket clips, three trace clips, several belly and neck clips and one full clip. The thickness and cleanliness of the horse's coat will make a difference to how quickly the blades become blunt.

11. A circuit breaker will cause the electricity supply to the clippers to be cut off if there is a problem. This is a safety measure, to make sure that both horse and human are protected from electrical faults.

12. It is generally best to begin clipping on the horse's shoulder. This is a flat area which is uncomplicated to clip and, being near the front of the horse, you are clear of the horse's hind legs should it kick out. The shoulder is also a less ticklish area, so the horse isn't likely to become upset or irritated.

13. In September and October, the horse's winter coat will be fairly well grown. Therefore, this is usually when the first clip of the winter months takes place.

14. Some more common breeds of horse grow very thick summer coats. If this is the case, and the horse is required to work quite hard, it may help to clip the summer coat.

15. It is helpful to have an assistant to hold up one of the horse's legs while you are clipping awkward areas like the elbows. An assistant can also encourage a horse to stand still, or help you match the height of lines – when working on a blanket clip for example.

16. Sometimes, a horse may become fidgety when ticklish areas are being worked on or towards the end of the clip. An assistant can hold up a leg to encourage the horse to stay still, or take a pinch of skin on the neck, or the horse may need to have a twitch applied.

17. If the person clipping the horse does not take the necessary care, the horse can easily become frightened. For example, if the blades are allowed to become too hot they will burn the horse and if the person is careless in handling the clippers the horse's skin could be nicked. Both burning and nicking will cause pain and the horse will thereafter associate clipping with being hurt. This could lead to problems next time the horse is clipped.

18. When clipping the area at the top of the tail, a small triangle of hair is left to make a neat finish. This will ensure that the hairs themselves are not damaged. When the leg hair is left on, as for a hunter clip, the muscle lines at the tops of the legs are followed, to make a neat finish. They can be left high or low, depending on the horse's conformation thus improving the horse's appearance. When the horse's head and face are clipped, some of the face hair is left on if the horse dislikes being clipped in that area. If this is the case, the bridle line is followed to give a pleasing appearance.

19. When the clip is completed, the horse can be "hot towelled". A towel is soaked in very hot water, then wrung out as much as possible. The towel is then wiped across the horse's coat; it lifts grease, scurf, and loose hair left behind after the clipping process. This gives the horse a smart appearance and cleans it up before rugs are put on.

20. While clipping, it is important to keep the horse warm. As the coat is removed, the horse is gradually being exposed to the cold. A spare blanket can be used to cover up the newly-clipped areas and help to keep the horse warm. It is also important to keep the horse out of draughts.
21. The clipper blades should be removed after use. The blades and the clippers should then be separately and thoroughly cleaned. As an added protection, the blades should be wrapped in oiled paper and the clipper head in oiled cloth. Blades and clippers should then be stored away in a clean, dry, warm place.
22. The horse's ears, chin and lower jaw line, and feathers, can be trimmed.
23. To trim the ears, gently squeeze the edges of the ears together; then trim off the excess tufts of hair, level with the outer edge of the ear. Take a pair of scissors and trim the long hairs from the lower jaw line as close as possible to the skin. To trim the feathers, use a comb to bring the feather hair up, thin cut the hair across the comb as close as possible. Work your way up the feather hair until it is all trimmed and a neat appearance has been achieved.
24. In this illustration, the comb and scissors are being used to make a neat finish when trimming the horse's feathers.
25. The horse has some long whiskers around its muzzle and over its eyes which are there to act as feelers. Some people prefer to trim them away, thinking that the horse will then look smarter; other people believe that the horse needs its whiskers and do not trim them.
26. The native breeds of horse and pony are generally left with full manes, tails and feather hair. It is thought correct to present them in their most natural appearance.
27. To pull the horse's mane you need a mane-pulling comb. Comb out the mane, so it is free from tangles, then begin at one end and take a few of the longest hairs, push the other hair back and take a grip as near as possible to the roots of the long hair. Twist the hair around the comb, then with a quick jerk pull the hairs out. The hairs must come out by the roots and not be broken. Work your way along the mane until you have reached an even length that you are pleased with. Some horses' mane hair comes out

quite easily. If a horse is warm, and its pores are open, the hair will come out more easily.

28. Once the mane is pulled, it can be plaited easily, so owners who wish to plait their horses for showing and competition need to pull their horses' manes. Also, very long manes can easily get in the way when the horse is being ridden. Many people pull the horse's mane so that they can ride without it getting caught up and in the way.

29. The horse's mane needs to be pulled to quite a short length. Say, no more than 15 cm (6 in) long. It needs also to be well combed out so it is free from tangle.

30. It is helpful to have something to stand on when plaiting. You will need elastic plaiting bands or needle and plaiting thread, a comb and a body brush with some water to dip it in to. The horse needs to be tied up, then you should be ready to begin.

31. Begin plaiting from the poll and work down to the withers. If you then have any straggly hairs left at the end, which cannot be fitted into the plait, they can be trimmed off or concealed under the front of the saddle.

32. You can only plait full tails, not ones that have been pulled. The tail needs to be full and in good condition with plenty of long hair growing from the very top.

33. To plait the horse's tail it is useful to have an assistant, who can help to keep the horse still. The tail needs to be well groomed and free from tangles. An elastic band or needle and plaiting thread will be needed to secure the plait at the end, and you need some water to damp the tail hair with.

34. To plait a mane, you can divide the mane into a number of bunches, or use the width of your mane comb as a guideline for each bunch as you work. Plait the selected section of the mane, then secure the end with an elastic band or with a thread. Roll up the plait so that it forms a small ball, and secure with another elastic band or with thread. The idea is to end up with an even number of plaits including the forelock plait, and for each to be even in size. To plait the tail, damp the top hairs, and select some small sections from each side of the dock, as high as possible, and from the very underneath tail hairs. Bring three sections together to form a plait, and keep the plait as tight as possible. Progress by

adding in further sections of hair and plait down the dock, finally plaiting the hair into one long plait at the end and secure it with an elastic band or with thread.

35. When pulling the tail the idea is to remove some of the tail hair to leave a slim line top to the tail for a neat appearance. To achieve this, work down each side of the tail, pulling out, by the roots, excess tail hair from underneath so as to leave a smooth appearance on top.

36. In this illustration, the assistant is holding up the horse's tail so that the person cutting the tail can see at what level the tail will be carried when the horse is active. In this way, the tail can be cut to a suitable length, making it look neat but not too short.

Chapter 6: **The Horse's Health**

1. Ten points can be selected from the following. Clear, bright eyes. An alert expression. A shiny coat. Normal temperature. A well-furnished body. Droppings normal and regular. Supple skin. Eating and drinking normally. Salmon pink mucous membranes. Urine pale yellow in colour. Normal response to capillary refill test.

2. Ten points can be selected from the following. Discharge from eyes and/or nose. Looking dull and uninterested. Coat staring. Raised temperature. Very thin or very fat. Droppings loose, hard and irregular. Skin slow to relax if pinched to test elasticity. Not eating or drinking. Mucous membranes pale, yellow, or red. Urine very dark in colour. Capillaries slow to refill if tested.

3. Apart from good general stable management practice, the horse should be "wormed" on a regular basis, have its teeth checked at least once a year, and be vaccinated against influenza and tetanus.

4. Keep records of when the horse was last shod, wormed, vaccinated, and had its teeth checked. In this way you can ensure that you are prepared for when the horse is next due for any of these procedures.

5. This horse is being given a worming dose.

6. If the horse has a large wound that may need stitching or checking for further underlying damage, or if the horse is lame, or if the horse has abnormal temperature, or if the horse is displaying signs of colic, it would be a good idea to call the vet.

7. A sick horse requires a comfortable and quiet environment. If rugs are needed, they should be lightweight. The groom should make frequent visits, but with a minimum disturbance, to check on the horse. Light grooming, only, to keep the horse comfortable, but not to disturb it or let it get cold. Small feeds should be given, and a plentiful clean water supply provided. Records should be kept of the horse's condition, and treatment given.

8. To detect lameness, walk the horse in a straight line on a firm even surface, away from you, then back towards you. Repeat in trot. Look for the horse nodding its head down when one particular limb takes weight. This shows which leg the horse is using for support, and the opposite leg is therefore the one being saved because of pain.

9. The horse has a bright and alert expression. It appears to be free moving. The horse's body is well furnished and not too fat. There are no obvious signs of injury or blemish.

10. Whilst there is ongoing research into this topic, it is generally accepted that a horse should be wormed every six to eight weeks.

11. The horse's teeth should be checked twice a year.

12. If the horse has had difficulty chewing, and has been seen to be "quidding", or if the horse appears uncomfortable with its bit, or if it is drooling excessively, it may well need attention to its teeth.

13. If a horse has been lame, it should not be ridden again until it is completely sound and has had one or two days' further rest. If it has been sick, it must be completely recovered and be eating and behaving normally again before it is returned to work.

14. Horses' teeth continue to grow and are worn down by the action of chewing. As the teeth wear down, sharp notches often form on the edges of the teeth. These notches can cause the horse discomfort and cut into their cheeks. The rasping of the horse's teeth removes these sharp notches and makes the horse comfortable again.

15. A horse not wormed may carry a very high worm burden. This can cause colic, irreparable gut damage, and general unthriftiness.
16. First, remove the cause. Bathe with salt water, dry and apply a soothing ointment. Once heeled, harden the skin with surgical spirit and make sure that clean, soft girths are used to prevent reoccurrence.
17. If the sore is in the corner of the horse's mouth, bathe it with salt water and apply Vaseline. If the sore is inside the mouth, wash out with salt water. In both cases, do not use a bit until the sore is healed.
18. A superficial cut should be hosed clean, then dried with sterile cotton wool, then an antiseptic ointment or wound powder applied.
19. An area of heat and swelling can be cold-hosed several times a day. Support the limbs with bandages.

Chapter 7: **The Horse's Digestive System**

1. Lips – gather the food. Teeth – the incisors are the cutters, then the molars grind the food. Tongue – moves the food from the front to the back and sides of the mouth, then forms a portion of food into a "bolus" ready for swallowing. Salivary glands – saliva is discharged into the mouth through tiny openings. It makes the food wet and warm and contains enzymes that start to help break down the food. Epiglottis – blocks the entrance to the trachea to ensure that the food passes down the oesophagus only.
2. The horse's stomach is approximately the size of a rugby ball, but expands to accommodate 9–18 litres (2–4 gallons). The cardiac sphincter muscle controls the outlet. Gastric juice, containing enzymes and acid, is added to the stomach to aid digestion.
3. The small intestine has three parts: the duodenum which is about 1 m (3 ft) in length; the jejunum, about 20 m (65 ft) long; and the ileum, which is about 2 m (6 ft) long. These three parts of the small intestine can hold approximately 50 litres (11 gallons).

Fluids from the liver and pancreas are secreted into the small intestine to help break down food, while some nutrients are absorbed into the bloodstream. Peristalsis, muscular contractions, takes place to move the food along. The large intestine is formed in three sections: the caecum, the large colon, and the small colon. The caecum holds about 35 litres (8 gallons) and acts as a holding chamber for the next chamber, the large colon, which is some 3–4 m (10–13 ft) long and holds up to 80 litres (17.5 gallons). From the caecum and the large intestine water is absorbed, while bacteria break down cellulose in the food. This break down can take several days. The next section, the small colon, is some 3–4 m (10–13 ft) long and holds up to 16 litres (3.5 gallons); here, water and nutrients are extracted.

4. The alimentary canal is the name given to the entire digestive tract running from lips to anus.
5. A. Oesophagus. B. Liver. C. Stomach. D. Small intestine. E. Large intestine. F. Caecum. G. Heart.
6. A. Windpipe. B. Lungs. C. Diaphragm. D. Liver. E. Stomach.
7. The liver and pancreas.
8. The liver secretes bile which helps with the digestion of fat. The pancreas secretes digestive juices.
9. Carbohydrates supply the horse with energy.
10. Proteins are used for body building.
11. Horses cannot regurgitate food. The cardiac sphincter muscle acts as a one-way valve and prevents this from happening.
12. A. Molars. B. Incisors. C. Pharynx. D. Oesophagus. E. Stomach. F. Small intestine. G. Large colon. H. Caecum. I. Small colon. J. Rectum. K. Anus.

Chapter 8: **The Skeleton**

1. Knowing about the skeleton helps us to be aware of bony areas, so we do not damage them, and to tell us if there may be underlying damage should we find a wound on a horse.
2. The skeleton is the framework around which the horse's body is built. Without it the horse would have no rigidity.
3. Immoveable joints, like those in the skull. Slightly moveable

joints like those in the backbone. And freely moveable joints like the plain, hinged, pivot, and ball-and-socket joints.

4. The appendicular skeleton consists of the limbs.
5. The skull protects the brain, parts of the ears, eyes, and nasal passages. Also, along with the lower jaw bone it houses the teeth.
6. The vertebrae are the bones of the backbone and they protect the spinal cord.
7. The horse has 18 pairs of ribs. Of these, 8 pairs attach directly to the sternum and are called "true" pairs, while the other 10, "false", pairs are only attached to the sternum by cartilage.
8. The horse does not have a collar bone. The front limbs are only attached by muscles, tendons, and ligaments.
9. Cartilage is a smooth, flexible substance found in joints, where it helps to prevent friction.
10. A. Scapula. B. Humerus. C. Radius. D. Carpus. E. Cannon. F. Pedal bone. G. Navicular bone. H. Sesamoid bones. I. Splint bones. J. Pisiform bone. K. Ulna. L. Patella. M. Tibia. N. Short pastern bone. O. Long pastern. P. Tarsus. Q. Os calcis. R. Fibular. S. Femur. T. Pelvis.
11. A. Occipital. B. Facial bones. C. Mandible. D. Lumbar vertebrae. E. Scapular. F. Rib cage.
12. The stifle of the horse is equivalent to the human knee, the hock, the human heel, and the knee the human wrist.
13. The axial skeleton consists of the skull, spine, ribs, and sternum.
14. 7 cervical vertebrae. 18 thoracic. 6 lumbar. 5 sacral. And 15 to 20 coccygeal.

Chapter 9: **Horse Behaviour**

1. The most dominant horses will make themselves known, by chasing away the horses lower in the "pecking" order.
2. In order to make sure that all horses receive some food, several more piles of hay than the number of horses should be spread out in the field. In this way, when horses lower in the pecking order get chased away, they can move off to another pile of hay and away from the dominant horses.
3. The term "pecking order" comes from the way chickens peck at

each other to establish an order of the most dominant member down to the lowest member.

4. If the weather is very wet and windy a horse without adequate shelter will soon become cold and miserable. It should be brought in. Similarly, in very hot weather, a horse without shade or relief from flies could become distressed. It, too, should be brought in.

5. In the spring and early summer, mares will come into "season". This attracts the attention of geldings and kicking and fighting may ensue. To prevent horses injuring themselves or others, it is usually best to separate mares and geldings if there are several of each.

6. Horses that are relaxed in their field may lie down in warm, sunny weather.

7. If the horse is lying down on a wet and cold day, especially if it is away from other horses, there is cause for concern that something is wrong.

8. In this picture what appear to be two young horses are fighting. They are probably both male and trying to establish a hierarchy between themselves.

9. A horse left alone in a field, would probably become distressed. It would canter around and neigh, and run up and down the fence line and run to the gate. It may even try to jump out of the field so that it can find its friends.

10. Horses behave in this way when left alone because they are herd animals. It is their natural instinct to follow, and stay with, the herd. When left alone, a horse will look for the rest of the herd and try to follow them.

11. This is a display of aggressive behaviour, with one horse going to bite and the other returning the bite with a kick. It is the sort of behaviour seen when a more dominant horse goes to move the other horse away and the horse lower in the pecking order is making a token objection.

12. When a new horse is introduced to an established group, there will be a lot of cantering around, squealing and some kicking. This behaviour results from the group wanting to meet the horse and establish where it will fit in the pecking order. The new horse will also want to explore its new surroundings and find out

where the water is and where its boundaries are.

13. The stabled horse should be in the company of other horses – preferably near a horse with which it gets on. The horse needs to see out of its stable and to be able to observe anything that is going on nearby. The stable area should be fairly quiet, so that the horse is not upset by sudden noise or commotion.

14. A relaxed horse, happy in its stable, will eat and drink quietly, sleep, lie down, and greet you normally.

15. An unhappy horse would not settle to eat. It would rush around its stable and push at the door in some distress. It may whinny when approached and have a distressed demeanour.

16. Some horses like to be in a quiet area whereas others like to be where a lot is happening. This depends on the character of the individual horse.

17. A new, distressed, horse is likely to stand at the stable door and push as if it is trying to get out. It may neigh and rush around its stable. And, it may also turn its hindquarters towards you should you approach it or try to go into its stable.

18. If a stabled horse lays its ears back, or turns its hindquarters towards you, proceed with caution.

19. In its natural state, a horse roams free and can take flight from danger. Once stabled, the horse is confined and cannot take flight if it is frightened.

20. Approaching the horse quietly and offering food, will help to gain its confidence. You should talk to it quietly and be gentle. Make no sudden movements and keep your demands simple.

21. Expect the horses to cease grazing, raise their heads, and take flight away from the direction of the noise. They will group together to protect the foals and then, after moving off a short distance, will stop and turn towards the direction of the noise. Here, they can assess if there is any danger.

22. A fresh and excited horse will probably jig a little. It might also try to buck and kick out and is also likely to be more "spooky" than usual.

23. Ill-fitting tack is likely to cause pain, therefore the horse will show some discomfort. It may pull, lay its ears back, and kick out.

24. To gain a horse's confidence, be calm, quiet, smooth with your

movements, and be positive. The horse should not feel that you are nervous in any way; it should feel that you are in charge, but not aggressive.

Chapter 10: **Fittening**

1. A horse which has been at grass in the summer, needs to be introduced to spending time in the stable again. It also, gradually, needs to be introduced to hard feeds again. So a routine of bringing the horse in from the field, to stand in and have a small feed needs to be started. The period of time in can gradually be lengthened. Regular grooming also needs to begin, a light summer sheet can be used to prepare the horse for a rug and improve the coat. A farrier's visit will need to be organised, so the horse is shod ready for when ridden work begins. Vaccinations, teeth, and worming dates should be checked, so these things can be done, if necessary, before work begins.

2. A horse which has had a winter holiday has probably been having hard feed and been brought into the stable daily. More attention needs to be paid to the removal of the winter coat, and the gradual reduction of rugs, as the temperature improves. The same vaccination, worming, and teeth checks need to be made. A farrier's visit will also be needed.

3. When the fitness programme begins, the horse will only be on walking exercise and could become cold while being ridden, if it had been fully clipped. So leave clipping until more active work begins.

4. In the first week, the horse should have been have walking exercise. Start with 20 minutes and increase to an hour, fairly quickly, unless the horse is recovering from injury. The walking exercise should be purposeful, with the horse in a good outline. Walk on firm, level ground to begin with.

5. To prevent sores, apply surgical spirit, or salt water, to key areas. The girth area, over the back, behind and around the ears.

6. When working uphill a horse has to use its hindquarters and top line muscles; these are some of the most important of the horse's muscles. It also has to work harder, without having to work for longer, which is beneficial to the fitness programme.

7. This horse is being lunged, using a lungeing roller, rather than a saddle and bridle. This is a useful way of giving some general exercise and work to help the horse's suppleness. In the early stages, this can help to strengthen the horse without the added complications of carrying a rider and tack.

8. If the horse is worked correctly, the hindquarters and top line muscles are developed much more than if the horse was just left to itself. You will also be strengthening muscles, tendons and ligaments.

9. A horse recovering from illness or injury must be taken very gently and slowly when returning to work. The site of the injury, or symptoms of illness, must be carefully monitored, to make sure the horse is coping with the work given. Trying to progress too quickly may result in further injury.

10. The term "outline" refers to the shape in which the horse is working. It is very important, as only through the horse working in the correct outline can the necessary muscles work to be undertaken.

11. Working a horse in heavy going can result in tendon strain, or overreach. Working too fast on the roads can result in concussion injuries. Working on stony ground can cause bruising, especially bruised soles. Working on uneven ground can cause strains and twists.

12. In general, a horse will work for a good hour each day, sometimes longer and sometimes for not so long. It depends upon the type of work undertaken.

13. It can be a good idea to split the horse's work. It depends on the type and character of horse, and on the individual persons' work commitments.

14. Canter work usually begins after approximately four weeks, if the horse is progressing as planned.

15. It is always a good idea to introduce some schooling, whatever the horse is being prepared for. Schooling makes the horse a better ride and helps to improve its handler's control.

16. At the beginning of the fitness programme, the horse probably does not need a day off, but as it works more intensively it will benefit from a more relaxing day.

17. The horse illustrated is working in a good outline. It is carrying

its head and neck in gently raised and rounded outline, with its face nicely vertical, showing good acceptance of the bit. The hindquarters seem well engaged and the pace looks active.

18. When a horse begins work, especially if it has just come out of the stable, it needs a gentle warming up period to help start its muscles working properly. As with human beings, those muscles that have not been properly warmed up can be damaged.

19. It will take about 6 to 8 weeks, depending on how fat and "soft" the horse was to begin with and whether any injuries or setbacks are encountered on the way.

20. As the programme progresses and the horse is asked to work harder, with fitness increasing, the feed will be changed to less roughage and more concentrated feed. This will give the horse more carbohydrate for energy and more protein for body building.

21. Possible ailments would be bruised soles, knocks and brushes, and maybe strains.

22. The horse should always be cool and have its breathing rate returned to normal, before it is returned to its stable for checking over and so on.

23. The horse should be offered water straight away, but only be allowed to drink a little. Continue allowing small amounts at approximately 3 minute intervals, until the horse appears to have quenched its thirst. Then leave the horse with a full bucket of clean water, in the usual way.

24. The horse should be washed down so that it is possible to see clearly if the horse is free from injury, and so the horse is comfortable. Check carefully for any signs of injury, and attend to any minor scrapes. Call for a vet if anything more serious is detected. The horse's feet should be carefully checked. Make sure that the horse has feed which is easily digestible, water, and a comfortable stable. Check the horse has adequate rugs for the time of year.

25. The next day the horse should be checked for soundness by leading it out in hand and trotting it up. The legs should be felt and checked for any signs of heat and swelling. The horse should be given a day of rest, preferably in a safe paddock, with a companion if possible.

26. Lungeing is an alternative method of exercise which can help to give the horse variety in its work and keep it interested. For the rider/trainer it can save time when necessary, as 20 minutes' lungeing can be equal to an hour of ridden work. Lungeing can also help to improve the horse's balance and suppleness.

27. To rough-off for the winter, keep rugs light. Allow the winter coat to grow. Reduce hard feed, and increase the bulk feed. Cease working the horse, if you have adequate turnout facilities, and turn the horse out for gradually longer periods each day. Stop thorough grooming, to allow some grease to accumulate that will provide the horse with warmth and protection. Have the shoes removed, or just hind shoes if the front feet are not very strong. Check vaccinations, worming and attention to teeth again. Have any of these procedures done if they are due.

28. For a summer holiday, the horse's winter rugs will need to be gradually reduced. If there are adequate turn out facilities, the concentrate feed can be gradually reduced and replaced with longer periods of grazing in the field. Again, remove shoes and attend to vaccinations, worming, and teeth. When the horse is spending most of its time out in the field, choose a warm, pleasant period of weather and eventually leave the horse out all night and all day. Continue with the usual checks and care of the field-kept horse.

Chapter 11: **Grassland Management**

1. Horse paddocks should have a good, dense, even growth of grass and be free from weeds. To keep them in this condition, paddocks should be rested periodically, be kept clear of droppings, be harrowed from time to time, and be rolled when weather permits.

2. Fencing must be strong and constructed of materials that will not cause harm to the horse. The top bar or strand of wire should be approximately 1.25 m (4 ft) high, depending on the size and type of horses, and the lower bar or wire approximately 46 cm (18 in) from the ground. A third bar or strand is needed between the two, to prevent horses from trying to climb between the two, or

two bars can be used if set closer together. If post and wire are used, the wire must be kept taut and not be allowed to sag. If rails are used they must be fixed to the inside of the posts to prevent horses pushing the rails of the posts when leaning on them. If electric fencing is used, it must be kept taut and be regularly checked to make sure that it is working properly.

3. In the top picture, the rails appear strong and well spaced. Fixed to the inside of the posts, they will resist horses leaning on them. A hedge has been planted a good distance from the fence. This will provide a shelter in the future, act as an added barrier, but be out of reach of the horses so they cannot harm the hedge. In the bottom picture, there is a good hedge, but the gate is badly broken down which would allow horses to escape, and it poses a hazard as the horses could injure themselves on the ragged bars.

4. The gate must be wide enough to allow easy access for farm machinery, so the field can be rolled and harrowed as necessary. The gate should open inwards, be well hinged so it swings easily, and have an easy to use catch that the horses cannot open. If close to a road or public path, the gate should be padlocked as an added security precaution.

5. A self-filling water trough is the best way of measuring a constant supply of water in the field.

6. The water supply should be checked daily and at every visit to the field. In the winter it must be checked to make sure it has not become frozen over and that the piped supply has not frozen. At all times water must be checked for debris; sometimes dead animals are found in water troughs, and in the autumn leaves may cause a problem.

7. Horses require shelter from wind, heavy rain, strong sun, heat, and flies.

8. Trees and hedges give natural shelter, or a purpose-built, three-sided shelter can be provided.

9. The plant pictured is ragwort. It is very poisonous to horses.

10. Foxgloves are tall plants with a thick main stem. Purple flowers grow at the top of the tall stem, in a series of bell-like shapes.

11. Yew is a bushy, dark, evergreen tree with very short needles rather than leaves. It has small red berries in the late summer/autumn.

12. Laburnum is a tall tree with fairly pale green leaves and yellow flowers which hang in clusters.

13. Deadly nightshade is a plant that grows up 1 m (3 ft) high. It has fairly dark green, oval-shaped leaves. The bell-shaped flowers are tinged with mauve.

14. A. Laburnum – a tree most often found in gardens. Watch out for laburnum in or near a field, along the edge of or near the fence line. B. Yew – a tree that can be grown as a hedge. Yew are often found in churchyards or, again, in gardens. If in or near a field, they may be found near to the edge, as part of the hedge itself, or where the field borders on to a garden. C. Foxgloves – these tall plants grow mainly in wooded areas but can also be found in gardens. They are most likely to be found around the edge of fields, near hedges and trees. D. Ragwort – a tall plant which grows at random in any area, so it may be found anywhere in a field. Often found growing on verges by the roadside. E. Hemlock – another tall plant. It tends to grow on verges and on the edge of woodland or close to hedges. F. Buttercup – grows all over the field mixed in with the grass. G. Deadly nightshade – a plant which tends to appear in hedges. Would almost certainly be found around the edge of a field which has hedges for its borders.

15. The fencing of horse paddocks should be checked daily, to ensure that nothing is broken on which a horse could injure itself and/or which would allow a horse to escape. Paddocks should, continuously, be checked for poisonous plants and trees and cleared daily of droppings. To allow grass a period of re-growth, paddocks should be rested before the grass is grazed too short.

16. Fences, gates, and the water trough should be checked daily. Checks should also be made for litter, in case anything has blown into the field, or been dropped there by a passer-by.

17. Field-kept horses should be checked as frequently as possible, but at least twice a day. This is necessary because, for example, a horse could be kicked and injured or tear its rug at any time. If something like this happens, action needs to be taken as soon as possible to prevent further injury or complication.

18. Most fields will need to be rested approximately twice a year. This will depend on the weather conditions and also how many horses graze the field at any one time.

19. It is usually best to allow 0.4 hectares (1 acre) for each horse. This does not mean that you need a 2 hectare (5 acre) field for five horses, but it does mean you should have that area available to use for the five horses. This will enable you to move them around and rest areas as necessary.

20. Droppings should be collected to prevent the spread of worms and to keep pasture fresh for grazing. Collect droppings daily, if possible.

Chapter 12: **Feeding and Watering**

1. Horses have relatively small stomachs. In the wild, feed is taken in small amounts almost continuously. Feeding little and often is a method of keeping as near as is possible to horses' natural way of grazing. By doing so, digestive problems should be minimised.

2. Poor-quality feeds do not contain the necessary nutrition for the horse and if dust is present in the feed it can cause respiratory problems.

3. Horses are creatures of habit. They quickly learn to expect to be fed at their regular times each day. Horses produce saliva in preparation for their feed, so if the feed is not forthcoming the result may be digestive upsets.

4. The horse's body is approximately 70 per cent water. Therefore, they need a good supply of water for all their bodily functions. A constant supply will help them to function normally.

5. (i) Feed according to the horse's age. Young horses need different levels of nutrients in their diet to that of older horses. (ii) Feed according to the rider's ability. For example, if a horse is fed large amounts of energy feed and its rider is too much of a novice to give it sufficient work, the horse is likely to become too difficult to handle for that particular rider. (iii) Feed according to the time of year. In warm, summer weather, with a good supply of fresh grass, the horse is not likely to need so much energy feed. Whereas, in the winter, the horse needs more feed to help keep it warm and to replace the lack of grass. (iv) Feed according to whether the horse is stable-, or grass-kept. If stabled, the horse

relies on what it is fed. At grass, the horse may obtain most of its nutritional needs from grazing. (v) Feed according to the horse's temperament. A relaxed horse is often a "good doer", and may not need so much feed. A highly-strung horse often needs more feed, as it burns up what it eats through nervous energy.

6. (i) Feed something succulent every day. Horses enjoy carrots and apples and so on, which help digestion and provide vitamins and minerals. (ii) Do not make sudden changes to a horse's diet; the bacteria in the hind gut help to digest specific foods and if new feed is introduced will take time to change. (iii) Do not feed directly before exercise. The stomach lies close to the lungs and if full will interfere with breathing during exercise. (iv) The horse's digestive system is designed to process plenty of "bulk" feed of the kind that horses will eat in the wild; bulk will help to keep the system working well.

7. Self-filling water troughs are best in the field. They provide the most reliable way of supplying water continuously, although one drawback is remembering to clean them out frequently. Other forms of water container, such as buckets, are filled manually and are likely to be knocked over or forgotten or become contaminated with dust and bedding. However, if checked and filled frequently, they are a good way of providing fresh, clean water to the horse and are frequently used in stables. Automatic water bowls provide a continuous supply of water and are labour saving, but they are often taken for granted when it comes to cleaning them out or checking that they are working properly. Again, they can become contaminated with bedding and droppings.

8. A bran mash is made by putting approximately 0.9 kg (2 lb) of bran in a bucket. Then add enough boiling water to make a crumbly consistency. Cover and leave to stand and cool off. A bran mash may be given to a horse thought to be unwell, or having a day off, or where it has just completed some hard work.

9. A bucket or similar container, is half filled with sugar beet shreds, then filled to the top with water. It is then left to soak for 12 hours. A bucket, or similar container, is one third filled with sugar beet cubes, then filled to the top with water. The mix is then left to soak for 24 hours.

10. Oats are a high-energy feed, containing mainly carbohydrate and being low in calcium. Barley has a similar feed value, but tends to be more fattening than oats. Sugar beet is a feed high in fibre. It provides energy and is succulent and tasty for horses.
11. Bran is a feed high in fibre. It is low in calcium and high in phosphorous, which is not a good balance for horses.
12. Horse and pony nuts/cubes must be fed with plenty of water available. Occasionally, a horse may choke on this type of feed if it eats too quickly.
13. The small bowl contains sugar beet, the larger bowl soaked sugar beet. And then, clockwise, the bowls contain: alfa-A; horse and pony nuts; bran; and coarse mix.
14. In this illustration, a horse is being weighed on a weighbridge. It is a useful exercise, enabling the calculation of quantities of feed to give to a horse. The weighbridge is also useful in calculating dosages for wormers and other medicines.
15. Coarse mixes are feeds made up of a selection of different grains and nuts containing added vitamins and minerals. These mixes have feed values specially formulated for certain horses. For example, you can buy a coarse mix for young horses, for old horses, for brood mares, for horses in hard work, and so on.
16. A horse's appetite is equal to approximately 2.5 per cent of its body weight. The horse's body weight can be assessed on a weighbridge, or with a weight tape, or from a weight chart. The amount of feed can then be calculated and slightly less than calculated should be fed. Select feeds according to the normal rules of feeding.
17. A sick, or resting, horse should be given low-energy bulk feeds, such as hay and bran mash.
18. By feeding soaked hay or haylage, and well-dampened concentrate feeds, you can minimise the dust around a horse and help prevent respiratory problems.
19. A young horse needs more protein for body building and growth than does an older, mature, horse.
20. Horses and ponies out in the field in the summer, should have a plentiful supply of grass and therefore not need supplementary feeding. In winter, when grass dies back, the horses will need hay and hard feed to make up their nutritional requirements.

21. A feed chart helps to make sure that horses are given the correct amounts of feed daily. If different people are involved in the feeding routine, they can check against the chart to see what individual horses are to have day to day.

22. The names of the horses, the number of feeds per day, the different types of feed, and the quantity of each feed for each horse, are the main items to put on the feed chart. There may also be additional notes on various extras and additives that individual horses are to be given.

23. Hay can be a quite dusty feed, even if it is of really good quality. By soaking hay, dust is eliminated and horses with respiratory problems can then be fed the hay without being exposed to any harm.

24. The hay can either be put into a haynet, then into a tub, or directly into a large tub. The tub is filled with water and the hay is left for an hour or so, to absorb the water. Then, excess water is drained away and the hay can be fed.

25. Haylage, or "horsehage", can be fed to horses. Packed in semi-wilted form into plastic bales, this hay is moist and dust-free. One problem with feeding haylage is that once the bales are opened they do need to be consumed within a limited amount of time, otherwise mould starts to form. Some varieties of haylage are much higher in energy content than others and, for some horses, it is too rich. However, good points are that the horse has a dust-free, high-quality feed which provides a consistent level of nutrition. Storage is often easier, as the bales do not have to be completely under cover, and usually smaller quantities are delivered at any one time.

26. Whole barley can be boiled to make a warm and tasty feed that helps to put on weight and condition. It is especially useful in the winter, if you have a horse which is under weight and in poor condition.

27. To prepare barley for feeding, place approximately 0.45–0.90 kg (1–2 lb) in a large saucepan. Fill the pan with water and bring the mix to a boil. Turn it down to a simmer, and leave simmering gently for several hours, or until the grains have swollen and burst open. You may need to top up the water level during the simmering process to prevent the mixture from boiling dry.

28. Flaked and micronised barley has been cooked in its preparation process. This makes it more digestible for the horse. Rolled barley is just the whole grain broken open.

Chapter 13: **Travelling**

1. The horsebox or trailer should be positioned in a quiet area, where other horses and people will not be passing during the loading process. If the horse is likely to be reluctant to be loaded, park alongside a wall or a hedge so that the horse cannot try to walk round the loading ramp and will have to go up it.
2. Travelling bandages, or travelling boots. Overreach boots. A tail bandage and tail guard. A light rug. A leather headcollar and poll guard.
3. An alternative to knee and hock boots with bandages is travelling boots. They offer all-in-one protection to the horse's limbs, from above the knee and hock, right down to below the coronet band.
4. A. Poll guard. B. Leather headcollar. C. Knee boots. D. Hock boots. E. Travelling bandage. F. Tail guard.
5. Poll guards are made in different designs. Some just protect the poll, and others cover the top of the head and incorporate protection over the tops of the eyes. It is used to protect these vulnerable parts of the horse during a journey. When being loaded for a journey, and while travelling, the horse is in a confined space with low headroom. It could easily hit its head if it threw its head around if frightened, which may cause injury and more fright.
6. If there was an accident and the horse became somehow caught up, it would be better if the headcollar broke, letting the horse loose inside the box. Headcollars made of synthetic materials can be almost unbreakable. Whilst leather headcollars are strong, they will break under more extreme stress.
7. The weather on the day is an important factor, but also consider how many horses are travelling together. In the enclosed space of a horsebox, the horses can generate a great deal of heat and quickly become too hot. Also consider the other equipment worn. Boots and bandages will keep the horse warm as well.
8. A tail bandage is not always necessary and, if the journey is too

long, could be harmful. Not all horses rub their tails when travelling and a tail guard can be used as an alternative.

9. The bandage on the left would be the one to use for travelling. It extends right down over the fetlock and coronet band and will protect the horse if it loses balance and treads on itself during a journey.

10. A tail guard is a piece of material that wraps around the top of the tail to protect it during a journey. It can be used with or without a tail bandage. Some horses lean back on their hindquarters during a journey and, in so doing, rub the top of their tails. A tail guard prevents this from happening and at the same time protects the top of the tail.

11. These are travelling knee boots.

12. Travelling knee boots are used to protect the horse's knees, in case it should fall while being loaded or unloaded during a journey. The boots should be fitted with the top strap quite tight above the knee, so they will not slip down, and with the bottom strap quite loose so that the horse can bend its knee without restriction.

13. Hock boots provide protection for the hocks when the horse is in transit. Some horses rub their hocks against the back wall of the horsebox while travelling. This makes it necessary to have protection for this vulnerable area. The hock boots should be fitted with the top strap quite tight above the hock, to prevent the boot from slipping down, and with the lower strap left quite loose so that the horse can flex its hocks.

14. If you wish to protect the horse's knees and hocks, but do not have boots, adequate protection can be given, using large pieces of fybagee underneath travelling bandages. The fybagee can be made to protrude well above the bandage, so it covers the front of the knees and the back of the horse.

15. Use the minimum amount of equipment. There is then less for the horse to get caught up in and less to frighten it should something come undone or break.

16. Travel boots are very quick and easy to put on. However, they do not provide the horse with support. Bandages are a little more difficult to put on, but they provide the horse with good support for the journey.

17. Overreach boots can be useful for travelling, as they protect the very lowest extremeties of the horse's limbs and hooves. When travelling, the horse can easily lose balance and stumble sideways, treading on itself and causing injury. The overreach boots can provide some protection under these circumstances.

18. It is a good idea to make sure that the horse is familiar with the travel equipment you intend to use. If the horse has not worn boots and bandages before, it may find them frightening. Well before the day of the journey, therefore, fit individual items of equipment on the horse. Let the horse get used to them in the stable and then lead it around the yard until the horse appears to be at ease. The horse should then be relaxed about wearing the equipment in future.

19. It is usually best to equip the horse just before leaving. Many horses learn that travel equipment means a journey which might excite and upset them.

20. The handler should wear gloves, strong footwear, and a hard hat for protection. If a horse plays up and objects to going in the horsebox or trailer, accidents may happen, so be prepared.

21. The handler should lead the horse in a straight line and in a purposeful walk towards the horsebox. The horse needs to feel that the handler is confident. Never turn and look at the horse, or try to pull it into the loading vehicle; just walk beside the horse and look ahead.

22. A reluctant horse will sometimes be more confident if another horse is loaded first. Feed in a bucket can tempt many horses. Bringing a lunge line around a horse's hindquarters can help to encourage it forward. The most important thing is to give the horse confidence.

23. Before the trailer ramp is lowered, the handler should be with the horse and have it untied. If using a front unload trailer, encourage the horse to stand quiet while the ramp is lowered. Then lead the horse slowly forward, and try not to let it rush. Some horses like to stop at the top of the ramp and look about. The handler should allow the horse to do this, then lead them on down when they are ready. If it is a rear unload trailer, the handler should go in and untie the horse before the ramp is lowered, then encourage the horse to stand still as the ramp is lowered. An assistant

should lay a hand on the horse's hindquarters to reassure and guide it, as the horse is backing out into an area that it cannot see. Both handler and assistant should try to keep the horse calm and steady and prevent it from rushing. Once the horse has backed out far enough so that it can see its surroundings, it may want to stop and have a look around. It should be allowed to do so.

24. Begin by lowering the horsebox ramp. The handler should then go in and untie the horse. An assistant then turns the horse towards the ramp and should try to keep it slow, so it steps carefully down the ramp. Once again, if the horse stops to look around, allow it to do so.

25. A trailer has a very low ramp and most horses find this easier to cope with. If it is a front unload trailer, it is possible to open up the trailer and give the horse confidence that it is not going into a closed box. However, the small space in a trailer can be off-putting to some horses. A horsebox offers more space, which is encouraging for the horse, but the steep ramp can put them off wanting to go in.

26. If the horse rushes, or tries to jump down the ramp, it may injure itself by falling, going down on its knees, or coming off the side of the ramp.

27. You might check to see if a horse is too hot or, possibly, too cold. Also check that the partitions are secure and any equipment the horse is wearing is correctly in place.

28. The driver of the horsebox should take care to slow down in plenty of time at all junctions and their like, so that there is no sudden applications of the brakes. He or she should also avoid low branches, which could scrape along the top of the horsebox and maybe frighten horses inside. Care must be taken to negotiate corners and bends very slowly so that the horses are not thrown off their feet.

Chapter 14: **Lungeing**

1. A. Side rein – to give the horse a contact to work into and to help keep it straight and balanced. B. Lunge cavesson – provides a secure point of attachment for the lunge line, so that the handler

can carry out the task safely. C. Lunge line – allows the handler to keep control of the horse on a circle, while asking the horse to work around. D. Brushing boots – this type of boot protects the horse from knocks and bangs to its lower limb if it should lose its balance. E. overreach boots – this type of boot protects the coronet band and heels, in case the horse should tread on itself while working.

2. You would lunge a horse to give it some exercise, to help improve its balance and suppleness, and to teach it basic commands if it had not yet been hacked.

3. Working a horse on the lunge for 20 minutes can be equivalent to riding it for one hour. So, depending on how fit the horse is at the beginning of a fitness programme, you may lunge from 10 to 20 minutes. Most work on the lunge is done at trot, with short periods of walk to warm up or wind down, and short periods of canter if need be.

4. The horse should always be asked to walk away from the handler when moving off onto a circle. It should be kept at a walk and be discouraged from rushing off straight into trot.

5. The handler should wear strong footwear, gloves, and a hard hat. These are needed for protection, as horses can become strong and excitable when on the lunge. The handler is vulnerable when down at floor level with the horse.

6. When lungeing, the handler should be aware of his or her own balance. Step left leg forward and around the right leg when on the right rein – and vice versa when on the left rein. The lunge line should be held in neat coils in the left hand when lungeing on the left rein and vice versa on the right rein. The lunge whip should be kept low, and follow the horse around the circle, so that the handler is the apex of a triangle: the horse the base, the lunge line and lunge whip the two sides. The horse should be kept out on a minimum of a 15 m (50 ft) circle.

7. There is no need for full tack every time. There may be a reason why the horse cannot wear a saddle or bridle and, if the rider does not intend to ride the horse, the full tack is not necessary.

8. The handler should wear protective clothing. If more than one horse is in the arena, the handler should not crack the whip, as it might startle other horses. When other horses pass the horse

being lunged, they should keep to the same rein. Always lunge in an enclosed area: if the horse tries to take off, the handler would not have a hope of holding the horse.

9. Yes, it is useful as part of a fitness programme. It can save time on days when time is limited and it can provide variety in the horse's work.

10. Using a saddle helps to give the horse a sense of discipline. It also helps to keep the horse's back and girth area accustomed to the equipment.

Chapter 15: **General Knowledge**

1. Always slow to a walk. Make your presence known in a tactful manner. Pass at walk quietly, giving a wide berth. Be polite, and say good morning/afternoon.

2. Do not ride on private property or on footpaths. Ride around the edges of fields with crops in them, so you do not cause damage. Do not ride through livestock, as this could cause damage to both livestock and horses. Never trot or canter around blind corners on roads and tracks, as you cannot see if your way is clear.

3. Take great care when passing any houses, as sudden movement – for example, in a garden, behind a hedge – can cause horses to take flight. Leave gates as you find them, unless it seems obvious that livestock are escaping; in which case, locate the farmer/manager and ensure that they are alerted to the problem. Avoid busy roads whenever possible, for safety's sake.

4. Don't ride on verges, as there may be many hidden items (such as broken bottles); once on the verge you have no escape margin if cars come too close. Ride on the left-hand side of the road, the same as the traffic. Keep mainly to walk, only trotting if the road is straight and clear, or if you help the traffic by trotting out of the way. Roads are slippery and horses unpredictable, so you are safer keeping to walk. Keep to single file, unless the road is wide and straight, when you can move in double file. Thank all drivers who slow down for you. Take care to be alert for hazards, so you can keep your horse under control and avoid accidents.

5. First, keep calm. Make the scene of the accident as safe as possi-

ble. This includes halting the ride, sending someone for the loose horse (if there is one), and someone else for help as necessary. Whilst all this is being done, approach the injured person. Speak and reassure them. Tell them to remain still. Check them for injury and stem any obvious bleeding. If they are alright, let them get up if they feel ready to do so. Make sure they are steady on their feet. If the person has banged their head, do not let them remount. If they are unconscious, check their airway and breathing. Keep talking to them, it may help bring them round. Put them in the recovery position if they are in danger of choking. Send for an ambulance but do not leave them alone. After any accident make a record in the accident book of what has happened.

6. If an accident occurs on a road, try to make sure the loose horse is caught as soon as possible, so that it does not cause further accidents. Do not allow the rider to remount if he or she is not fully fit to do so; they may fall off again and cause further injury. Try to keep the rest of the group calm so they do not panic and cause more problems.

7. If the person doesn't have any obvious injuries, but has hit their head and feels sick and shaky, the recovery position is the safest option. Also, if the person is unconscious and in danger of choking they should be put in the recovery position.

8. The British Horse Society (BHS) has a board of trustees at the head of its structure.

9. There are a number of different sections. Membership, Riding Schools Approvals, Education and Training, Examinations, Access and Rights of Way, Hunter Trials, Welfare, Safety, and Rescue and Rehabilitation.

10. Membership benefits include free information leaflets, membership facilities at major shows, BHS Visa card, free personal liability and personal accident insurance, and legal, tax, and rating help lines.